"Ronnie Floyd combines the passion of an evangelist and the compassion of a successful pastor. He also has the ability to share these passions in both his speaking and his writing. You will not be the same after reading this book!"

—DR. TIM LAHAYE
Author of best-selling series, *Left Behind*

"What a passionate and perfectly timed message for our generation of Believers. Dr. Floyd is a gifted pastor-teacher. A true man of God. We have much to learn at his feet."

—BETH MOORE
Speaker, Teacher and Writer

"With a Space Shuttle, before there is lift off, there must be ignition. Similarly, in the Christian life, there must be ignition, before there is lift off. This book is for you if you want the ignition to lift off and reach new heights in the Christian life."

—DR. TONY EVANS
Senior Pastor, Oak Cliff Bible Fellowship, Dallas, Texas
President, The Urban Alternative, Dallas, Texas

"There is nothing so cold as a fire that has gone out. And, there is nothing so empty as a heart that has lost its passion. Dr. Ronnie Floyd gives us key disciplines that can change a smoldering Christian into a believer whose heart is ablaze. I believe his book will be a spark for personal revival that will, in turn, be used to ignite a new generation of 'on-fire' believers."

—JANET PARSHALL
Nationally Syndicated Talk Show Host

"There has never been a time in our nation's history when we needed spiritual reformation more than at this time. Life On Fire *will be used by God to ignite many flames and hopefully a nation ablaze for Christ.*

—DENNIS RAINEY
Executive Director, Family Life

"How many of us have wished, at one time or another, that our relationship with God was more powerful and relevant. In his new book, Life On Fire, *Dr. Ronnie W. Floyd guides us back to the fundamental spiritual disciplines that will revitalize our walk and life from his own powerful, personal life and ministry."*

—DR. BILL BRIGHT
Founder and President, Campus Crusade for Christ International

"Some authors write better than they live. Ronnie Floyd is a man who lives out what he writes and speaks. His is a life on fire for Jesus Christ and out of that life he has written a book that informs the mind and inflames the heart. No matter where you are in your journey with Jesus, this book will stoke the fire of your relationship."

—DALE SCHLAFER
President, Center for World Revival and Awakening

"Ronnie Floyd's ministry is not only proven absolutely trustworthy, but his life is aboundingly fruitful. He's a sower—sowing both the truth of the Gospel, as well as of the wisdom of God's Word—sown into believers who want to grow."

—JACK W. HAYFORD, D. LITT.
President/Pastor, The King's Seminary, The Church On The Way

"The present generation of Christians seems to have forgotten the disciplines of the Christian life. As a result, too many Christians are living in spiritual defeat, compromise, and deadness. Pastor Ronnie Floyd, whose passion for the disciplines of the Christian life has so shaped his ministry, here offers practical guidelines for recovery of authentic Christian discipleship. May God use this book to call His people to repentance."

—R. ALBERT MOHLER, JR.
President, The Souther Baptist Theological Seminary

"Ronnie Floyd's life and ministry is a blazing illustration of what he writes about in Life On Fire . . . God indeed uses the spiritual disciplines to ignite the fire in our lives for Christ and His Cause . . . This book will stoke the fire in your soul."

—DR. CRAWFORD W. LORITTS, JR.
Associate U.S. Director, Campus Crusade for Christ

"This book is not a discourse from an armchair philosopher. Both the author and the church where he serves epitomize the truths that are so clearly delineated. God knows that in these days of apostasy, apathy and "painted fire" we need reality. Surely, this book helps to meet that need. I commend it."

—DR. ADRIAN ROGERS
Pastor, Bellevue Baptist Church, Memphis, Tennessee

"Ronnie Floyd is ablaze with God's glory! His new book ignites the soul with spiritual passion. It is must reading for anyone who wants to experience the power of God."

—JERRY FALWELL
Chancellor, Liberty University

LIFE
ON
FIRE

RADICAL DISCIPLINES FOR
ORDINARY LIVING

RONNIE FLOYD

WORD PUBLISHING

NASHVILLE

A Thomas Nelson Company

To Mike Shillings,
my friend in ministry and former pastor,
the first person I saw who lived a
Life On Fire.

Thanks for letting God use you to
set me on fire!

Unless otherwise noted, Scripture quotations are from the New American Standard Bible (NASB). Copyright © 1960, 1977 by The Lockman Foundation. Used by permission.

Other Scripture references are from the following sources:

Holy Bible: New International Version® (NIV). Copyright © 1973, 1978, 1984 by International Bible Society. Used by permission of Zondervan Publishing House. All rights reserved.

The King James Version of the Bible (KJV).

The Message (MSG). Copyright © 1993. Used by permission of NavPress Publishing Group.

Library of Congress Cataloging-in-Publication Data

Floyd, Ronnie W., 1955–
    Life on fire : radical disciplines for ordinary living / Ronnie Floyd.
      p. cm.
    Includes bibliographical references.
    ISBN 0-8499-3748-5
    1. Christian life. I. Title
    BV4501.2.F5735 2000
    248.4—dc21   00-061457
                                                                         CIP

Printed in the United States of America

00 01 02 03 04 05 BVG 6 5 4 3 2 1

CONTENTS

CONTENTS

Chapter 1

I Want to See Fire

How would you describe your life: smolder and smoke, or deep embers and blazing fire? Or are you somewhere in-between?

Let me tell you about a friend. George was young and energetic, a very likable guy. One day, he called my office in deep desperation, and I rearranged my busy schedule to see him.

George had been married only five years when his wife, Susan, walked out on him. She had become very weary of his demanding job and his lack of sensitivity to her. When he arrived home from his demanding job, he would either head to the golf course or cruise down the cyberhighway.

When George walked into my office the day Susan left, he was a broken man. His heart was aching, and his emotions were uncontrollable. He knew he had a problem with his wife, but he also knew he had an even deeper problem.

Susan was a Christian, but George was simply religious. He came to church with her on the Sundays he could not play golf and heard me share about the value of having a personal relationship with Jesus Christ. George knew that he did not have a relationship with Christ.

That afternoon in my office, his gloom lifted when I had the joy of leading George to Christ. Peace took over the countenance of that broken man. The Lord transformed him right before my eyes!

George shared his experience with Christ with Susan, and he attempted to make things right with her. She regretted walking out on him and was grateful for his conversion. George was not only reconciled to God, but also to his wife.

There is more to this story. George was really on fire for the Lord. The people around him did not understand what had happened, but they noticed a significant change in George's life. The passion that once

3

was sold out to his career, golf game, and the Internet had been transferred to his relationship with God. George's life had been transformed.

Several months after George's exciting turnaround, he began to be weighed down with the normal day-to-day challenges in life: a busy schedule, a demanding job, unrealistic expectations, and family responsibilities. We have all been there. George was struggling in his faith, and his fire began to smolder.

I was between meetings on a very busy day when George called. He insisted on seeing me that day. After my final scheduled meeting, George sat across from me in my office. Once again I heard desperation in his voice, but this time his desperation had nothing to do with his marriage or job.

George went directly to the reason for his need to see me. I will never forget his words: "Pastor, I want to see fire!"

I was at first taken aback by his statement, but as he continued, I began to understand. "I have been a Christian for several months," George said, "and God has done some great things in my life. But everywhere I go, I meet Christians who are apathetic about their faith. I'm afraid that I might become like them. I sense that my fire for God is going out. As I read the Bible, I see people who had the fire of God in their hearts."

Then he repeated the words that are etched forever in my mind: "Pastor, I want to see fire!"

I took this opportunity to encourage George from God's Word. As I shared with him, my heart was so encouraged by this young man's desire for his life to be a blazing fire for God. After I prayed with him and escorted him from my office, I sat down and kept replaying his words in my mind: "I want to see fire!"

You see, I have been where George was that day many times in my spiritual journey—times when I was not satisfied with where I was, when I wanted to go farther than others seemed to want to go, and when I wanted more of God in my life. One of those times occurred a couple of years ago.

It was the fall of the senior year of my oldest son, Josh, and football season was in full swing. Josh was a national record-holder as a quarterback that season. As his team continued its quest for the state championship, our lives were busy at every end of the spectrum.

As always, things were hectic in our lives. My ministry was full of constant demands and pressing deadlines, and my two boys had busy schedules that were taxing on all of us. But our family lived for high-school football and church activities. That was our life, and we enjoyed it!

There was only one problem. As November rolled around, I was distracted. I felt something was not right. My time with God was meaningful many days, but I was in a rut!

As I neared the end of that year, it all began to make sense to me. My fire was smoldering. I had unintentionally become distracted while handling the things of others and even the things of God. My family's busy schedule had caught up with me. I had little to give in my relationship with God because I was pulled in too many directions. I was so busy trying to fan everyone else's fires that my own fire was dwindling.

> I was so busy trying to fan everyone else's fires that my own fire was dwindling.

I knew that was not where I wanted to be in my spiritual life, and I did not want to stay where I was. I wanted to go farther with the Lord than I had ever been. Most of the people around me did not notice my spiritual struggle, but I knew I had a problem. I wanted more.

I did not say it as George said it, but his words were in my heart. I, too, wanted to see fire—not a smoldering fire, but a fire with deep, blazing embers in my life.

FIRE IS OUR EMBLEM

One of the ways people express themselves is through their clothing. In an effort to be perceived as "cool," some people wear clothing that is denoted by the company's emblem—a sign, an image, or a badge.

These emblems often appear on the front or back of a shirt, on a cap, or on the back pocket of jeans.

Here is how it works. In order to wear the company's emblem, you have to pay more money for their clothes. That emblem on your clothing then gains you various levels of acceptance within certain groups of people. I know it is strange, but true!

Like the emblems on a clothing company's products, there are many emblems of the Holy Spirit in Scripture. The Holy Spirit of God is the presence of God. Therefore, when you see an emblem of the Holy Spirit, it should immediately point you to God, just as a certain emblem on your clothing should point you to a certain company. For example, the Holy Spirit is described throughout Scripture in the emblems of wind, rain, water, oil, and a dove, among others.

One of the powerful emblems of the Holy Spirit is fire. The Holy Spirit is described in terms of fire more than four hundred times in Scripture. There are various meanings of fire in these verses. There are too many to share in depth, so I will share just a few, as seen in one passage of Scripture.

Fire As God's Presence

Moses was a great leader who was used mightily by God. The story of God's personal appearance to Moses is recorded in Exodus 3:2: "The angel of the LORD appeared to him in a blazing fire from the midst of a bush; and he looked, and behold, the bush was burning with fire, yet the bush was not consumed."

In God's personal encounter with Moses that day, He demonstrated Himself through flames of fire. Fire is seen in Scripture as representing the presence of God. This experience of being in the presence of God changed Moses' life forever.

Fire As God's Protection

The Lord surrounds His beloved people in order to protect them. This is seen in Zechariah 2:5: "'For I,' declares the LORD, 'will be a wall of fire around [Jerusalem], and I will be the glory in her midst.'"

God promised to surround the city of Jerusalem, the holy Zion, with a wall of fire, which represented His very presence. Though without walls, Jerusalem was going to be protected by the fire of God.

Fire As God's Purification

Once we have placed our faith in Jesus Christ, we are to live by faith. This faith will develop and grow as God takes us through the process of purification.

God uses the trials and circumstances of life as a refining fire. The Bible says, "These [trials] have come so that your faith—of greater worth than gold, which perishes even though refined by fire, may be proved genuine and may result in praise, glory and honor when Jesus Christ is revealed" (1 Pet. 1:7 NIV). Our faith becomes purified when we walk through the fiery trials of life.

Fire As God's Judgment

The judgment of God is seen throughout Scripture. His judgment comes upon those who oppose God's people. It comes upon God's people when they disobey Him. God's final judgment will come upon those who have never trusted in Jesus Christ and Him alone for their salvation.

In Hebrews 12:29, God's judgment upon sin is described as "a consuming fire." The judgment of God will be expressed with great force and fire upon those who have not chosen Jesus Christ as their Savior and Lord.

Fire As God's Indwelling in Us Personally

The way God relates to His people changed on the day of Pentecost. In Acts 2:3, the Bible describes the coming of the Holy Spirit in terms of fire: "They saw what seemed to be tongues of fire that separated and came to rest on each of them" (NIV). These flames of fire were God's verification that He had sent the Holy Spirit to be upon each believer.

In that moment, the Holy Spirit came to live within the lives of believers, never to leave again. In times past, the Spirit of God would come upon a person for an assigned task and then leave that person when the task was completed. Since the day of Pentecost, the Holy Spirit has come to establish permanent residence within the believer.

The fire of God, the Holy Spirit, lives in you. Pentecost marked the beginning of the indwelling of the fire of God within you.

Fires Don't Just Happen

Fires don't just happen. Before you can build a fire, the conditions have to be right, preparations have to be made, and materials have to be gathered.

I confess to you that I am not a Boy Scout, yet I understand some of the basics about building a fire. It is important that the ground beneath the fire is dry. Whatever materials you choose to use need to be dry as well. Fire is greatly hampered by dampened and wet materials.

Once the conditions are right and you have gathered the correct materials, you are ready to build a fire. You need to begin by placing several twigs together on the dry ground. If you see some dry leaves nearby, you can gather them and place them under the twigs. When you have arranged the twigs, ensure that there are passageways for the fire to receive oxygen. Place a few pieces of newspaper along these passageways. This will help penetrate the twigs and other materials. Finally, place small branches, logs, or pieces of wood on top of the twigs. Remember, if a fire is built properly, its life is certain; if built improperly, it will not burn.

> Remember, if a fire is built properly, its life is certain; if built improperly, it will not burn.

Now it is time to light the newspapers that have been placed along the passageways of the materials. Be sure extra newspaper is available to assist the fire in its beginning stages. Once the newspaper is lit, the fire begins to burn. In moments, the twigs begin to burn. In minutes, there is a synergy between the twigs as they burn together. As the twigs burn brightly, the branches begin to become a part of the fire. As the fire receives oxygen and proper materials, it burns brightly. However, no fire continues to burn successfully without the proper conditions and materials.

After a fire has burned an extended time, you will notice a couple of things. You begin to see ashes. They may still be somewhat hot, but they contribute little to the present fire. You will also see embers. Embers are pieces of wood at the base of the fire that have not all burned up but provide life to the fire. They may glow orange or red. They are so powerful you could not hold them in your hand. If you were to place your hands over the flame directly, they would be scorched. If you were to attempt to hold an ember, your hands would be scarred. The deeper the embers, the greater the fire!

If your fire begins to go out, you may be tempted to use anything handy to try to get it going again. If you are at a campsite, you may attempt to put an egg carton or a milk carton on the fire. The fire may quickly burn brighter, but the flames last for just a moment. The materials only provided a quick burn!

If you want the fire to burn powerfully again, the conditions have to be right and the right materials have to be added at the proper time.

ARE THE INGREDIENTS RIGHT FOR YOUR FIRE TO BURN?

At the moment of your salvation, the fire of God's Holy Spirit came to live within you. His fire, His presence, His Spirit indwells you.

For the fire of God to burn brightly through your life, it is necessary for the right ingredients to occur in your life every day. Just as the level of intensity of a real fire is determined by many conditions, the spiritual fire of God within you will only burn as brightly as the conditions of your life. The ingredients have to be right for the fire to burn with the greatest intensity.

Do you have twigs in your life that are wet? Are the leaves of your life damp? What about the branches of your life—are they dry and ready to burn? Perhaps the newspapers in your life have been outside catching the wrath of a storm. If any of these areas are dampened with the circumstances of life, the conditions are not ready for the fire within you to burn.

Rather than doing what is necessary for the fire to burn rightly within and through you, temptation may lead you just to apply something for a quick burn. A milk or egg carton will add a quick burn to a fire, but in moments it is gone. My friend, the same is true of spiritual materials that only provide a quick burn in your life.

A concert of your favorite Christian music group, a Christian CD, a conference on the Bible or on the family, a retreat, a camp meeting, a praise song, or even another Christian book (except this one) may provide you nothing more than a quick burn. It may fire you up for a day, a week, or more, but soon you are back to the same place you were before you experienced it. All of these quick burns have their place, but they are substitutes for what you really need.

You need something more. That "something more" is what this book is about. If you are looking for a quick burn, then give this book to someone else or put it on the shelf. But if you want to go farther than you have ever been with God, then embrace what I share with you in this book. If your heart aches with spiritual dissatisfaction, then read on. If you are ready to get out of the spiritual rut you are in right now, what you hold in your hand will show you the way out. If you are wandering aimlessly in your spiritual life, your spiritual navigation system is this book. Read the words. Internalize its truth. I guarantee that your life will never be the same.

You had better be ready, because the challenges are great. It is my desire that this book would call a new generation of Christians who are ablaze with God's presence and power—the kind of Christians who are radically different from the world. I don't mean different by being weird, obnoxious, and offensive; I mean different by living by the spiritual disciplines that will keep the fire burning regardless of the cost, the circumstances, or their feelings. When you live in and operate your life by these spiritual disciplines, they will ignite your life! You will never be the same again!

The deep embers of your fire are these spiritual disciplines. They will keep burning to provide the intensity for the fire of God in you, just as the deeper embers provide the intensity for a campfire.

The ashes that have fallen aside are the past spiritual experiences of your life. They were good to provide a quick burn but not good enough to last for an extended length of time. Though it was meaningful for the moment, yesterday's worship service will not cut it for today. Your spiritual experiences will help you learn and grow, but many times they are nothing more than quick burns that have diminished into the spiritual ashes that lie beside the fire of God in your heart.

The Christian life is not about ashes, but embers—spiritual embers that will ignite a flame for the world to see. I heard a statement years ago that comes to my mind today: "Get your church on fire, and the world will come and watch it burn!" My friends, if you will nurture the deep embers of these spiritual disciplines in your life, the world will come and watch you burn.

> The Christian life is not about ashes, but embers—spiritual embers that will ignite a flame for the world to see.

Some May Need to Fast-Forward to Chapter 14

Before you read on in this book, some of you may need to fast-forward to chapter 14. Why? The conditions and ingredients of your life are not right for your fire to burn. If the conditions are right when you read and embrace these disciplines, a fire will ignite that will change your life. But if you continue to read when the conditions are not right, this book will just join your heap of spiritual ashes. I do not want that to happen, and I do not believe God does either.

Therefore, if some of the leaves, twigs, and branches of your life are wet, you might want to detour for a moment to chapter 14. If you will, you will learn what to do when the fire goes out in your life. Take the challenge of this brief detour to chapter 14. When you have completed that challenge, return to chapter 2 in order to begin your walk through the disciplines that will ignite your life.

THE ANSWER

Regardless of where you are in your spiritual life, this book has what you need. If you are healthy, growing, and mature, this book will only add the proper fuel to the fire already burning within you. If you want to go farther with God than you have ever been, this book can help you.

Every Christian on this earth needs to have a *Life on Fire*. That is what this book is all about. Are you ready to learn how to set your life on fire? Are you ready to know what will keep fanning the fire in your life? Are you ready for me to share with you what will happen in your life when the fire burns? Tired of smoldering ashes and smoke? Let's go to higher ground!

When these spiritual disciplines become the deep embers of your life, your life will become a blazing fire. Press on, and take the journey of a lifetime!

CHAPTER 2

SETTING YOUR LIFE ON FIRE

Disappointment and discouragement are twin towers to scale in life. At certain times, they appear to be taller than life itself. Being close to Jesus does not always ensure that you will not be haunted by disappointment and discouragement.

Just ask Cleopas and his friend. They had heard Jesus teach and were closely associated with Him. Even though they were not part of the twelve disciples, Scripture verifies they were followers of Christ.

Cleopas and his friend were on their way to Emmaus, located only seven miles from Jerusalem. The tragic events surrounding Jesus' death still penetrated their hearts. It was only three days after Jesus was crucified. With great sadness, they were recounting how the Light of the World died on the cross. In the same way, the light of hope in their hearts had been snuffed out.

Cleopas and his friend were very disappointed. Like all those who had loved Christ and had followed Him, they were plagued with gloom upon their hopes and dreams. Jerusalem was cloaked with this spirit of depression. Cleopas and his friend had genuinely believed that Jesus was going to be the Redeemer of Israel. They were convinced that He would usher in a royal kingdom on this earth for the people of Israel. Their dream had been shattered just three days earlier.

Drowning in the sorrow of this disappointment, their hearts were aching with discouragement. What was next? Would they be alive when the true Redeemer came? They were in deep conversation, reviewing the truths Jesus taught and reliving the events of Jesus' life and death. Rehearsing His words in their minds only resulted in more questions and greater grief over His death.

Please understand, Cleopas and his friend were aware of other evidence while exchanging this provocative dialogue. That very morning, before they left Jerusalem, people had claimed that the stone had been rolled away from the entrance to Jesus' tomb. They had even heard that the tomb was empty! Reports buzzed among Jesus' followers that two angels of the Lord had told the women attesting to these things that Jesus was alive! Even Peter testified that when he went to check the tomb for himself, he found only the linen wrappings of Jesus. In addition to this incredible evidence, Cleopas and his friend were privy to many of the deep insights that Jesus shared, including the prediction of His own death, burial, and resurrection.

Rather than perceiving that God was up to something very special, they could not grasp that Jesus came as a suffering servant, not a royal king. What seemed like a biblical and theological error kept them from seeing the real truth right before their eyes.

While Cleopas and his friend were walking toward Emmaus, Jesus appeared to them. He entered immediately into their deep dialogue, but they did not recognize Him. Jesus asked them what they were talking about because they appeared to be so sad. Cleopas asked the man he did not recognize as Jesus, "Where have you been? Are you not aware of the events that happened just three days ago in Jerusalem?" Jesus responded, "What things?" Cleopas recounted to Him the events relating to Jesus' death, the reports of the empty tomb and the angels' appearance to the women, and how their dream of Jesus reigning as king of Israel had been shattered.

Cleopas was blind to the truth because of disappointment, discouragement, and what seemed to be a biblical error. He had no idea that he was talking to Jesus, the very One he was talking about.

When Cleopas was finished with his exposé on the matters at hand, Jesus said, in essence, "You guys are so slow!" He asked them why they did not believe what the prophets had written about Jesus—that Jesus needed to suffer before He entered His glory. The Master Teacher, Jesus Christ, began with Moses and continued through all of the prophets, explaining to them how the Law and the

Prophets spoke of Jesus and His coming to earth to die and then be resurrected.

Can you imagine what it must have been like to hear Jesus Himself explain how He was revealed in all of the Scriptures? This would have been the most incredible Bible conference anywhere in the world. I would give anything to have listened to Jesus explain these matters.

Cleopas, his friend, and Jesus arrived at Emmaus. Cleopas and his friend asked Jesus to stay with them for the evening. The moment Jesus blessed the bread and began to give it to them, the lights came on! Their eyes were opened, and they recognized Jesus! As soon as this occurred, Jesus vanished from their midst. Listen to what they said when they realized it was Jesus with whom they had been speaking: "Were not our hearts burning within us while He was speaking to us on the road, while He was explaining the Scriptures to us?" (Luke 24:32). Their hearts were set on fire by the words of Jesus and the Word of God that He explained to them.

As soon as this happened, they ran to Jerusalem to share with Jesus' disciples that they had seen Jesus. Upon their arrival, before they could say a word, the disciples informed them that Jesus was alive and had appeared to Simon. Cleopas and his friend began to verify this truth by relating their experience to the eleven disciples of Jesus and others. This fascinating story is recorded in Luke 24.

The disappointment and discouragement of Cleopas and his friend vanished. Their hearts were on fire! Now it all made sense. Jesus' death was necessary for God to demonstrate His power through the resurrection. This plan was God's plan to save the world, and their lives would never be the same again. Little did they know that, in just days, the fire of the Holy Spirit would come to live within them permanently.

On this unforgettable day, Cleopas and his friend learned that having Bible knowledge only gives you a "big head," but receiving Bible truth and walking with Jesus will set your heart on fire. Warren

Wiersbe said it best: "Understanding Bible knowledge can lead to a 'big head' (1 Cor. 8:1), but receiving Bible truth and walking with the Savior will lead you to a burning heart." Wiersbe is one of the great Bible scholars of our day, yet even he cautions you not to be captivated by Bible knowledge alone.[1] Knowledge only leads to arrogance, rather than authentic spirituality.

The American church is full of obese, knowledge-filled Christians. The smorgasbord of Bible studies offered by all kinds of groups would make one think that the key to the Christian life is knowledge of the Bible. Yet for many of these people, the fire of the Spirit ranks from minimal to nonexistent. If you are a "knowledge-driven" person, you need your heart to be set on fire.

You can be a star at Bible trivia, yet your heart can be as cold as ice. You can stand to teach God's Word in various settings and do so without the passion of God's fire. It happens every day, especially on Sundays, all around the world. Some of the people who are most unfriendly to the spiritual things of God are filled intellectually with Bible knowledge. A person may fight over biblical issues and yet be just as blind over the supernatural activities of God.

> You can be a star at Bible trivia, yet your heart can be as cold as ice.

Learn from Cleopas and his friend. The power of God comes alive when you are receiving the truth of God in Scriptures and living it out in your life. Moving it from your head to your heart will set your life on fire.

I do not know if disappointment has smoldered God's fire within your heart or if discouragement has robbed you of vitality and fire in your life. Maybe these twin towers do not plague you at this moment, but you may experience many other detractors like these. Every one of them will dampen the fire in you.

You need your heart set on fire just as Cleopas and his friend did. In the following section, I will briefly outline several actions that will set your life on fire.

Actions That Will Set Your Life on Fire

In order to escape the dryness of Bible data, you must commit to taking a few necessary actions. Without these actions, I would be like dry bones. However, through these actions, I have been able to stay fresh in my walk with Christ and my ministry. Therefore, I commend them to you.

Investigate the Truth About Jesus Christ

One of the reasons that Cleopas and his friend were filled with such disappointment was that the Jesus they had imagined was not the real Jesus of the Scriptures. This is why Jesus spent the trip to Emmaus teaching them how He was revealed in the Scriptures. Their knowledge of religious tradition and lack of personal study of the Scriptures blinded them to the truth before their eyes.

A wrong view of Jesus will dilute the real Jesus. Be careful you have in your mind the real Jesus when you search for truth in the Scriptures. When you make decisions in life, make them with an authentic view of Jesus, rather than a view in contrast to the Jesus of the Scriptures. One of the reasons people are caught up in extremes in various areas of Christian living or error concerning the Bible is that they have not investigated the real truth about Jesus Christ. How is this accomplished?

Search the Scriptures

The Bible is our guidebook for life. The Bible is our source of authority. The Bible reveals the one true God and unfolds the entire truth about Jesus Christ from beginning to end. The life of faith that each one of us has been called to live is determined by the Word of God. This is why Romans 10:17 says, "So faith comes from hearing, and hearing by the Word of Christ." Therefore, we must search the Scriptures in order to live by faith.

Searching the Scriptures begins with *reading God's Word*. You simply cannot compromise this spiritual discipline in your life. The only way you will ever come to the full truth of Jesus Christ is to read the Bible.

Knowledge of God's Word is essential in the Christian life. We need to be as committed to investigating the truth discovered in the Bible as an investigative attorney is in a high-profile murder case. Not one piece of evidence should be left unturned. But as previously warned, knowledge in and of itself is dangerous. But knowledge of God's Word coupled with the power of the Holy Spirit will ignite your life.

For at least a decade, I have read through the Bible every year. Nothing has been more beneficial to me. God speaks to me through the Bible. My knowledge of God's Word has grown and my faith has been enlarged through reading the Bible from Genesis to Revelation on an annual basis.

I want to challenge you to read the entire Bible during the next twelve months. There are many ways and many resources available to help you accomplish this worthy challenge. Do not think that reading through the Bible is an unreasonable goal. God will help you find a way to do it. I believe He wants you to do it. Do you want greater faith? Read the Bible!

Searching the Scriptures also involves *studying God's Word*. The Bible challenges us to do this in 2 Timothy 2:15: "Be diligent to present yourself approved to God as a workman who does not need to be ashamed, accurately handling the word of truth." The challenge is to be zealous and persistent in studying God's Word. We will not be able to properly interpret the Bible until we desire to discover truth with precision and accuracy.

One of your goals as a Christian should be to become a student of God's Word. You can develop the needed tools to rightly divide the Word of God. The market is abundant with resources that can help you learn how to study the Bible.

Studying the Scriptures will lead to the truth about Jesus Christ.

Study is a necessary discipline in life. Since we live in the information age, we may be content merely to watch someone else reveal the content of his or her studies. This is a very tragic mistake. No one else can walk with God for you. Another person's discipline cannot be your discipline. I urge you to study the Scriptures on your own. Once you discover its great truths for yourself, your life will be transformed, and you will be motivated to continue plumbing the depths of God's Word.

The outcome of reading and studying God's Word will be that you will see the real truth about Jesus Christ. You will become equipped so that false or distorted teachings about Jesus will become unacceptable to you. Your faith will mean more to you than ever before. In addition, your life will be set on fire. If you are going to have a life on fire, you must practice the discipline of investigating the truth about Jesus Christ through reading and studying God's Word.

One of the godliest people I know is a young man named T. Ray Grandstaff. T. Ray is the president of the Fellowship of Christian Athletes for the state of Arkansas. Through the years, we have developed a very good relationship. We occasionally meet to challenge, share, and encourage one another. T. Ray and I were recently discussing spiritual disciplines and the importance of reading God's Word. T. Ray shared with me that his goal for this year was to read the Bible through five times.

As I listened to him speak, I noticed that T. Ray's countenance, as always, was pleasant and direct, his eyes piercing with the love of Jesus Christ. I wondered, *Is there a connection between T. Ray's countenance and his discipline of reading the Word of God?* I believe the answer to that question is yes. T. Ray's life and countenance personify the Word of God.

If you are challenged by T. Ray's conviction, you too can find the time to read the Bible. You will spend your time on something. Why would you spend your time reading

> Why would you spend your time reading things like the newspaper, much of which is not true, rather than reading the Bible, which is all true?

things like the newspaper, much of which is not true, rather than reading the Bible, which is all true? Establish the spiritual discipline of reading the Word of God. When you do that, you will be positioning yourself to be used of God more than you can even imagine. What God is doing in the life of T. Ray Grandstaff is amazing; his future is God-sized. Your future is as bright as the promises of God. Go to the Word and read about those promises. You will never be the same again.

Learn from Others

One of the quickest ways to limit your thinking and to place yourself in the detour of error is to avoid learning from others. Learning from others can add much to your spiritual life. God shows each person who seeks Him various things about Himself, and we can learn from the insights God has given to other Christians.

Cleopas and his friend learned from Jesus in the same way. Remember, they did not even recognize Jesus, yet they learned so much from Him. They testified that their hearts were burning as He explained the Scriptures to them. The discipline of learning from others will set your heart on fire.

Learn from others who are skilled in God's Word. Learn from commentaries and Bible helps. Learn from your pastor. Learn from the teacher of your small group, community group, or Sunday school. Open your heart to people with whom you might initially disagree and listen to their biblical positions. Learn from godly men and women who are gifted with extraordinary biblical insight.

It is imperative that you filter what you learn from others through the Word of God. This is why it is important for you to read and study God's Word for yourself. Otherwise, you may be misled concerning an element of your faith. If you become zealous in this area, you will lead others down the wrong path.

If you want your life on fire, investigate the truth about Jesus Christ by searching the Scriptures and learning from others.

APPLY GOD'S WORD

Anyone can study the Scriptures in the same way a doctor would study the human body. The only problem is that study in and of itself may not always lead to spiritual vitality. This is why applying God's Word is so important. The application of Scripture takes the Word of God to a new level in your life.

Why should you do this? If you do not apply the Word of God to your life, someone or something else will become your authority. A person who only studies will in time become the authority in everything and may, over time, develop a mind-set that everyone else is wrong. This will lead to division in the body of Christ.

Another reason you should apply God's Word is that it is the only authority in life. Second Timothy 3:16 tells us, "All Scripture is inspired by God." The word *inspired* literally means "God-breathed." He spoke it in its entirety. Therefore, the Bible is an authoritative and perfect book that was breathed into existence by God. How could a perfect God do anything other than breathe something perfect?

When the Bible is your only authority for living, you will apply God's Word in your life. When you read or study Scripture on your own or listen to someone else expound it, you apply what you have learned. When you apply God's Word, your culture or circumstances will not determine your decisions in life. Your decisions will be made based upon the authoritative Word of God.

When Cleopas and his friend applied what Jesus had said to them, their hearts were set on fire. They were ablaze with His power!

There are several ways to apply God's Word in your life. Let me mention just a few.

Receive the Word of God

When you receive the Word of God, you embrace its truth—the truth of Jesus Christ. He is the First and the Last. When you receive the Word of God, you internalize it in your life.

When you are listening to someone else expound the Scriptures, follow this tip. While they are speaking, ask God, "What do You want to say to me through this teaching?" Then ask God, "How do You want me to apply this message in my life?" When you really receive the Word of God, you are taking steps of action on how to get it from your head into your heart and into your life.

Think upon the Word of God

One of the great ways to apply God's Word is to think upon the Scriptures. The Bible challenges you to meditate on the Scriptures. This means that you are constantly thinking upon them, even saying them over and over again in order to grasp their meaning. Concentrate, focus, and think upon the Word of God.

At times, after I finish reading a passage of Scripture, I just close my eyes and attempt to see and to feel the passage. I have thought for hours on the story of the disciples on the Emmaus road, the passage that serves as our foundation for this chapter. The more I think upon it, the more I understand it. The more I think upon it, the more I feel that I am on the Emmaus road, listening in on Jesus' words.

> Slow down. Do not get in a rush. Take the needed time to think upon the Scriptures. It will set your life on fire.

Slow down. Do not get in a rush. Take the needed time to think upon the Scriptures. It will set your life on fire.

Pray the Word of God

Another way to apply the Word of God in your life is to pray the Word of God. As you discover sections of the Scripture that relate to various areas of your life, pray them out loud to God when you are at that place in your life. It is powerful!

For example, if you feel that your heart is dealing with unrepentant sin, read Psalm 51 and pray it back to God. Get on your knees.

Go verse by verse, personalizing it as your prayer to God. This repentant psalm David voiced concerning his sin with Bathsheba can serve as a great encouragement for all believers as we pray about unrepentant sin. Applying the Word of God by praying the Scriptures will set your life on fire.

Memorize the Word of God

Scripture memorization is another powerful tool for setting your life on fire. It is very difficult not to live out what you have memorized in relationship to the Scriptures. Once you have memorized certain Scriptures, the Holy Spirit will bring them to your mind continually.

Many resources are available to assist you in Scripture memorization. For those of you who have young ones in your home, lead them to memorize the Word of God. It will be with them forever. Hardly a day goes by that the Spirit of God does not bring to mind various Scriptures I memorized when I was younger. Scripture memory will contribute to setting your life on fire.

Live the Word of God

Many people assume that applying the Word of God will automatically result in living the Word of God. I wish it were that simple. This is what I have found out in my walk with Christ. When I receive the Word, think upon it, pray it back to God, and memorize it, I am much more likely to apply it to my life. Each of these spiritual disciplines is necessary in your life.

After reading this chapter, will you take the actions stated to have your life set on fire? If not, then what value will your life have in the long run? It will probably be momentary, rather than long-lasting. If you do take these actions, you will live the Word of God I am sharing with you.

Establishing the discipline of applying God's Word will be beneficial to your life. Ultimately, it will set your life on fire.

WITNESS THE ACTIVITY OF GOD'S POWER

Another action that will set your life on fire is to be around people and places in which God is moving mightily. Cleopas and his friend learned this from being around Jesus. They were enlightened when He taught about Himself through the use of the Scriptures. They were energized when they thought upon all that Jesus had done through His miraculous bodily resurrection and His post-resurrection appearances to them. They were enthralled that God was working in their lives personally when they realized that they were talking with Jesus Himself. God had gotten involved with each of them, and their disappointment and discouragement disappeared once they realized Jesus was active among them.

Do not seek the miraculous; seek the God of the miraculous. If you seek Him, He will accomplish miracles in your life. When you can look at your life, witnessing the footprints of Jesus, you become inspired to live for Him. There is nothing like God working in your life in a powerful way. Is God doing a fresh work in your life? If so, let Him. If not, ask Him.

One of the secrets of witnessing the activity of God is to be in a church in which God is working mightily. I am not talking about numbers of people, crowds, and buildings; I am talking about being around a people upon whom God has set His fire, a people who are following God as He reveals His will to them. Find a church with a pastor who preaches the uncompromised Word of God and challenges you to go farther with God than you have ever thought about going, a pastor who is growing in his own walk with God and being blessed with the freshness of God's activity in his own life. Being involved in a church that is experiencing the activity of God will set your heart on fire.

Another secret of witnessing the activity of God is to have friends who are experiencing the movement of God in their lives, the kind of friends who call you to higher ground because of their intimacy with

Christ and the activity of God in their lives. God will use these friends to set your life on fire.

WALK WITH JESUS

The final step of action to set your life on fire is to walk with Jesus. Cleopas and his friend were set on fire by walking with Jesus to Emmaus. The power of what He was saying to them was expressed by His life. They were walking with the resurrected Christ, and it changed their lives forever.

Walking with Jesus in intimacy every day will set your heart on fire. Walk with Him in the morning as you start your day. Walk with Him while you are on your way through the day. Walk with Him in the evening wherever you may go. Read about Him in the Word. Talk about Him with your friends. Learn about Him from others. When you walk with Jesus, your life will be on fire.

A WORD ABOUT DISCIPLINE

Discipline occurs when you do what you should do even when you do not want to do it. Discipline calls you to do what is right, regardless if anyone else does. Discipline enables you to do what you know you should do even when the circumstances are not friendly to it. Discipline is essential in the Christian life. In fact, you will not live with fire in your life without practicing the disciplines I am giving to you in this book.

> Discipline enables you to do what you know you should do even when the circumstances are not friendly to it.

This book is about spiritual disciplines that will ignite your life. These disciplines will renew the fire within and give you back the freshness in your walk with Christ.

The first discipline of setting your life on fire involves understanding the place of God's Word in your life, witnessing the activity of

God's power, and walking with Jesus every day. Now you must determine to take some personal actions that will move these to a new level in your life. When you instill these spiritual disciplines in your daily life, God will set your life on fire.

Regardless of how much I work out in fitness and weight training, I have never gotten to the point where I just cannot wait to do it. Some days I would rather do anything other than work out. Yet, discipline calls me to it five to six days a week. When I leave the gym, I am so glad I made myself do something that I knew I needed to do but did not want to. The rewards are great in the short- and long-term of life.

The same is true in regard to implementing these disciplines in your life. Your flesh may cry out claiming its rights! The world will distract you from each one of these disciplines. Your enemy, Satan, will do all he can to keep you from instilling these disciplines in your life. Why? Because he knows they will renew your fire. The last thing he wants competing with his plan in the world is for you to have a heart set on fire. He knows he is defeated when this occurs.

So my friend, God wants to take you farther than you have ever been with Him as you place these disciplines in your life one at a time. Let these disciplines become the deep embers that will blaze with fire through your life.

Place these disciplines into your life because you know you need them, even when you do not feel like doing them. You will be so glad you did, because they will set your life on fire!

CHAPTER 3

MAKING GOD CHOICES

Let me introduce you to a real hero in the faith. He was a very old man when his final choice in life earned him the right to be recorded in the history books. He was the last leader still living in the year A.D. 168 who knew eyewitnesses of Jesus and heard them talk about Jesus' profound life and death. Most believe he was mentored in the faith by the apostle John. This elderly man's final choice in life was a God choice. His name was Polycarp, Bishop of Smyrna.

Charged with treason because he renounced Caesar and embraced Christ, Polycarp was brought before the Roman proconsul. Angry spectators filled the arena, readying themselves to see another Christian die. Under armed guard, the old bishop was brought before the bloodthirsty mob. The crowd was ecstatic when they learned the man who had been arrested and was now standing before them was Polycarp. This could be the day that the last living link to the apostles would come to an end.

The Roman proconsul attempted to compel Polycarp to embrace Caesar and to denounce Jesus Christ. With the arena full and the stage set for this showdown, everyone was interested to see what Polycarp would say. Would he concede to the proconsul's demand and be spared? Or would he stand by Jesus Christ and lose his life?

Polycarp was on the brink of making a God choice. He understood that this decision would either move him closer to God or farther away from Him. Every choice we make in life is a God choice.

On this day, Polycarp's decision was already made. Years earlier, he had decided that he was in the Lord's army and was going to stand by the banner of the cross. Therefore, when Polycarp was asked to curse Christ to save his life, he replied, "Eighty-six years I have served the Lord Jesus Christ, and He never once wronged me. How can I blaspheme my King who has saved me?"[1]

Polycarp was reminded that his life was at stake. Perhaps he was threatened with wild animals that would eat him. Without any reservation or uneasiness in his voice, he declared, "Let them come, for my purpose is unchangeable!"

Since Polycarp seemed unshaken by the threat of wild beasts eating him, the mob determined to kill him with fire.

Again Polycarp was not shaken. He reminded them that their fire would last for only a few minutes, while the fire of God's judgment against the ungodly would last forever. Polycarp was preaching his last sermon before this angry mob. He shared with them that they could threaten to kill him with beasts or with fire or any other method. He stated to them very courageously, "You shall not move me to deny Christ, my Lord and Savior."[2]

When they heard this, they knew that Polycarp had stood by his claim to be a Christian. They were moments away from getting their wish: witnessing another Christian execution.

The proconsul took immediate action to burn Polycarp at the stake. The crowd was raging. They said to one another, "What a fool of a man is this one named Polycarp!" Polycarp appealed to them not to tie him to the stake, but to leave him as he was to burn in the fire. They complied, tying only his hands behind his waist.

In the midst of this drama, Polycarp prayed, "O Father, I thank You that You have called me to this day and hour and have counted me worthy to receive my place among the number of the holy martyrs. Amen."[3]

The fire was lit. The flames rose high above his body. A miracle was happening—his body was not burning. He did not move. God was protecting this godly saint. Usually the stench of burned human flesh would fill the arena. Not this day! He was not burning. Finally, the executioner was ordered to kill the old bishop with the sword.

Polycarp was not shaken by the world, even at his death. Even though the sounds of hate and spite filled his ears at his trial, he still chose Jesus. The moment Polycarp died, the angels ushered him into the glory of heaven. I would think that a great reception took place that day when Polycarp modeled before the world the power of a God choice.

I believe it is very important to understand that Polycarp could not have died with such valor had he not lived with the same bravery. Somewhere in his life, he determined that he would be loyal to Christ, regardless of the pressures within himself, pressures by others, or pressures from the world. At some point as a faithful follower of Jesus Christ, Polycarp decided that he would not turn back from the direction he was going with Jesus. In clear terms, he was going on with Jesus all the way![4]

When this choice was made, Polycarp's life was set on fire—not by the wood from trees or the flames of human fire, but by the fire of the Holy Spirit of God who lived within him. The reason he did not fear human fire at death was because he chose God's fire in life. He was going on with Jesus all the way. To paraphrase the hymn writer, the cross was before him, and the world was behind him.[5]

This is a true God choice! One that is necessary to live by if you are going to be on fire for Christ. The spiritual discipline of making God choices says, "I won't turn back. My decision is made. I am going on with Jesus all the way. With every choice I make I am moving forward in my relationship with Jesus Christ." Just as an army charging forward into battle rallies to the flag at the sound of the trumpet, the army of God rallies to the cross at the voice of His Spirit in our lives. Through every decision, we are choosing Christ.

> Just as an army charging forward into battle rallies to the flag at the sound of the trumpet, the army of God rallies to the cross at the voice of His Spirit in our lives.

When I was fifteen years old, I repented of my sins and trusted Jesus Christ as my Lord and Savior. Immediately there was a change in my life. Within months, God called me into the ministry. I began to preach the truths of Jesus Christ. Yet my decisions were not all good decisions. I was still immature in my faith, but I was growing.

Just like many new Christians, I made some poor decisions even after I came to Christ and was preaching the gospel in my high school years. Yet, everyone knew I was different. My life had been changed. I talked about Christ and shared the gospel with others. God was moving in my life, and I began to attempt to live this spiritual discipline: "I won't turn back. I am going on with Jesus all the way."

Notice one key word in that sentence: *attempt*.

The day I was driving to college, I made my once-and-for-all choice. No longer would I turn back in any way. I was going on with Jesus all the way. When I wiped away the tears after leaving my parents and home, I had four hours to reflect upon my life and to ask God for His vision for my life. I had to leave the bondage of my past in Egypt so I could enter the Promised Land of going on with Jesus all the way.

Do not misunderstand me. Even though that day was the point of major decision for me, I have had to reaffirm that decision many times. I have never backed up since that day, but I have had to continually make choices in my life that reaffirm the decision I made on my way to college.

Those times of reaffirmation have come to me in all settings. I have reaffirmed that decision in my study when God revealed to me His message for His people. I have reaffirmed that decision in situations when I could have easily compromised but chose instead to go on with Jesus all the way. I have reaffirmed that decision when my children were pressuring me to permit them to do something because of the pressure they were feeling from friends, but I did not yield. I have reaffirmed that decision in conferences and seminars in which the pressure was on for acceptance, but I chose not to deny Him! I have even reaffirmed that decision in private when the pull of Satan was to watch a certain movie or explicit scene as I was surfing the channels, but I chose not to yield and instead chose Christ and His way of purity.

So I understand your pressure. I know what it is like as a leader. I know the pressures of being a parent. I understand the daily struggles that wage within you between the Spirit and the flesh. I know the pressures of the enemy. They have been on me in all kinds of ways while I am writing these words to you.

HAVE YOU MADE THIS CHOICE?

Where are you in making the once-and-for-all choice as a Christian not to go back to your ways in Egypt, but to press forward in going on with Jesus all the way? I realize that each person understands and implements this spiritual discipline at different points in his or her Christian journey. Have you made this choice?

Which way are the scales tipping in your life: toward God or away from God? Your life never lies to you. Look at your life. Do not listen to your words. Remember, every choice you make is a God choice that either moves you closer to God or farther away from Him. Where are you in the balance of this choice?

Backing Off

You may feel you have disappointed God so much by your poor choices that you are now backing away from the Lord. As a parent, you have backed away from quality time with God. As a spouse, you are inching closer toward sin with your coworker. As a student, your activities last weekend demonstrate that you are retreating from Jesus. Perhaps your Internet browsing has placed you into a chat room in which you are attracted to someone of the opposite sex. Yes, you are backing away from going on with Jesus.

There was a time in the life of the apostle Peter, one of Jesus' closest friends and followers, when he was backing away. As you study Scripture, you learn that Peter was a hotheaded, passionate disciple who often struggled with his own human weakness. With his words, he declared allegiance to Jesus, but with his life, he failed to uphold that allegiance. But Peter kept on trying. The ultimate picture of Peter backing away from Jesus was seen in his denial of knowing Him on three occasions at the events leading up to the crucifixion—a betrayal he deeply regretted.

That is exactly where backing away from a God choice will take you. Your life will represent mediocre commitment to Jesus. Your words may be strong, but your life is very weak. You need to set your life on fire. You need to implement this spiritual discipline of not going back, but choosing to go on with Jesus all the way. When you do, your life will be ignited for God like never before.

Close, but Not Sure

When Peter was warming his hands at the fire, he was physically close to the action. He could watch and listen to their deliberations about Jesus. Even though he was close, he was unsure whether to speak up for Jesus. He did not want to die! He loved himself more than Jesus, even though many times he had heard Jesus challenge him to deny himself, to take up his cross, and to follow Him. This night Peter was close, but he was unsure.

I believe this is where many Christians are in their walk with Jesus. They have tasted enough of the Promised Land to know it is good, but they still like the taste of the world. With one foot in the world and the other foot in their faith, they are so close, but just not sure. With one hand they hold their friends of the world, and with the other hand they hold their Christian friends. With one eye they gaze at the world, and with the other eye they glance at the cross. They are close, but unsure.

I know the world is attractive. It is very easy to love the world. You can see it, touch it, hold it, and feel it. Many times those things are great. I also understand the grasping power of the flesh, which yearns to be pleased continually. Quite honestly, many times the things

> Satan often makes his kingdom look beautiful. He offers enticing rewards if we will come his way.

of the world feel very good. Satan often makes his kingdom look beautiful. He offers enticing rewards if we will come his way.

Yet, I know there is another side of the story of the world, the flesh, and the devil. Once you are entangled by any of them, you may be entangled forever. Once you give in to your weakness, you may be saddled with massive consequences. I know that the world, the flesh, and the devil all lie because I have bought into their lies before.

Christians who are close to going on with Jesus wrestle more than people who have already made the choice to back away. Peter wanted to choose Jesus with all his heart that night, but he didn't. Failing to choose Christ caused Peter much grief and pain. That is exactly where you may be in your life.

Come on to the Promised Land. Once you are there with both feet, you will not want to go back to your bondage to sin. You will declare, as Polycarp did and as I have done, "I will not go back. I am going on with Jesus all the way." Make this decision today!

Moving Forward

I congratulate you for having made that choice prior to this moment or for making it right now in your heart. You will not regret going on with Jesus. The power of the Holy Spirit will see you through and help you to stand. Others in this exciting adventure will also help you to stand. Keep your eyes on Jesus, and remember the Polycarps of the faith! If they have done it, you too can do it with God's power.

Peter did. After being so close and then backing away in shame and denial, he made the right choice of going on with Jesus all the way in his life. On the day of Pentecost, the Lord appointed this man who had failed to be the first spokesman for the church of Jesus Christ. Peter's shame had turned into glory. His past was over. The future was bright—so bright that few have ever burned more brightly for Jesus. Legend has it that when Peter was sentenced to death by crucifixion, his final request was to be crucified upside down, since he felt he was not worthy to die in the same manner as Jesus. Peter died in the same way as he lived—sold out, not turning back, and going forward with Jesus all the way.

Keep going forward with Jesus. It will ignite your life!

PLEASE REMEMBER

Since every choice is a God choice that will move you closer to Jesus or farther away from Him, I want to go deeper on this subject for a few moments. I want to share with you what happens when you make a good choice and what happens when you make a poor choice.

The Power of a Good Choice

Each good choice you make in your life leads you to make other good choices. You will get on a roll! What do I mean? The power of making a good choice enables you to make other good choices.

My decision to go on with Jesus all the way led me to a reservoir of other good choices. While at college, I chose to be a student who would learn and grow. I also chose my lifelong sweetheart, who has been the perfect mate for my life and ministry. In addition, I chose to make some great Christian friends—godly friends who still challenge me to soar for God. I also made the choice of continuing my education at seminary, which was foreign to my thinking when I first arrived at college. There is power in making right choices.

I do not want to mislead you. The temptations were very great to go the other way. The flesh, the world, and the evil one pulled as much or more than ever before. They never gave up on their attempts to ensnare me. Somehow by the grace of God, the Holy Spirit gave me the power to say no and the power to say yes at the right times.

The Power of a Poor Choice

Every poor choice will always lead you to make other poor choices. That is the power of a poor choice. The reservoir of poor choices is similar to the one of good choices in that it is attractive and appealing; however, the reservoir of poor choices is also detrimental and deceiving.

The army of God is full of soldiers who have become like ashes in a fire. They were once contributors to the fire, but now they are just watching it burn. With the slightest wind they will blow away, possibly forever.

I have met people who made the same choice I am challenging you to make today. They said they would not turn back. They said they would go on with Jesus all the way. Yet now they are away from God and reaping the consequences from their poor choices. Some of them are laypersons who were once full of Jesus' love but are now far away from God. Others are ministers who started out with excitement and fire but are now piled in the ruins of poor choices.

The pull to Egypt was just too great for them. Perhaps the church was moving forward with a new, fresh, great move of God. They were in it with both feet. Then, possibly in their marriage, their spouses began to act like David's wife, Michal, who criticized David's worship after he danced alongside the ark of the covenant. He went a little too far with Jesus for her—at least farther than she wanted to go. Could this be you? Is it possible for this to be where you are in the balance—abounding in poor choices because one time you chose to step away? If you do not step forward with Jesus, you step away from Him.

> If you do not step forward with Jesus, you step away from Him.

The pull of Egypt is too great for many. The lure to go watch a movie with a sexual theme was just too great. Since that choice, your weekend pastime is going to the video store and bringing sexually explicit videos home where no one can see you, except God. For others, surfing the Internet brought a sexual image before you. Would you click or not? You clicked. Since that time, you now spend your leisure time on Web sites that fill your mind with lewd images. This leads to the chat room. The chat room leads to a relationship. The relationship leads to sex. Sex outside of marriage always leads to ruin!

Are you getting the point? One poor choice leads to many other poor choices in your life. What kind of choices are you making in your life today? Please remember: One poor choice always leads to another poor choice. And one right choice always leads to another right choice. Yes, every choice you make will lead you closer to Jesus or farther away from Him. Every choice really is a God choice.

WHERE NOW?

You may be asking yourself the following question: *If I choose to go on with Jesus all the way and never turn back, how does this play out in my life?*

Some of the most struggling followers of God were the Israelites in bondage in Egypt. Their hearts were characterized more by rebellion than surrender. In His boundless love, God led them out of Egypt through the leadership of His servant, Moses. According to biblical scholars, there may have been as many as two million people in this special group. They witnessed the great miracles of God that led to their exodus.

God had a mighty plan for this people. He had a special home for them known as the Promised Land. In spite of their reluctance, rebellion, and delays, God was committed to getting them where He wanted them to be. Exodus 13:21–22 records, "The LORD was going before them in a pillar of cloud by day to lead them on the way, and in a pillar of fire by night to give them light, that they might travel by day and by night. He did not take away the pillar of cloud by day, nor the pillar of fire by night, from before the people."

The pillar of cloud and the pillar of fire represented the presence of God. When the presence of God moved, they moved. By day and by night, God's presence was with them and guided them.

You have the same privilege that the nation of Israel had. In fact, you have more. You have the Holy Spirit of God living inside of you. You have the Word of God guiding you. This is why you need your life to be set on fire. God has a plan for your life. He has a destiny for you. He even has a way for you to get there.

So when you make the choice to go on with Jesus, never going back to your Egypt, you need to live that choice out every day. The two greatest challenges you face in living out this choice concern the will of God and the way of holiness.

The Will of God

Sometimes you probably wish that God would give you a pillar of cloud and a pillar of fire—it would simplify God's direction for your life so much! *Knowing* God's direction is helpful, but you still have to resolve in your heart to *do* God's will. This is where the battle is won or lost.

I am not quite sure that the will of God is as much about the place or the people as it is the process that God takes you through in the journey. You learn so much about yourself—the good, the bad, and even the ugly. Nothing brings this out quite like the crucible of decision-making.

I want to challenge you to get on your knees and tell God, "Lord, whatever, wherever, and whenever . . . the answer is yes!" Making that choice will lead you through the crucible of decision-making. Do not wait until you are in a dilemma. Do it today. That way, when temptation comes, your decision has already been made. You are just going to follow up on your choice to go on with Jesus all the way, never turning back. The follow-up concerning the will of God is saying yes before you know what "yes" is about!

Maybe you are single, and God has brought someone into your life. This person is exactly who you have prayed for; in fact, he or she is more than you ever expected. Yet you enjoy being single and are not sure you are ready to be tied down. What is God saying? Follow God.

Maybe you are a single parent and find that extra money is hard to come by. At the same time, you have been taught about the importance of giving. What is God saying? Follow God.

Perhaps you are in a marriage, and your spouse never spends time with you. You are ready to walk away even though you know God does not smile upon divorce. What is God saying? Follow God.

Maybe you are a working mom, and the pressures of marriage are growing daily. No one seems to appreciate all you do. You are ready to blow the top out real soon if things do not change. What is God saying? Follow God.

Perhaps the job you have always wanted has been offered to you. You are elated! The opportunity is great. The money is fabulous. The future is out of sight! You and your wife have continually prayed, asking God for this possibility one day in the future. Now you only have one problem: You live in Dallas, but the job is in Atlanta. You have a junior and a sophomore in high school. Your excitement pales every time you think about telling your wife and children. What is God saying? Follow God.

Once you have placed the spiritual discipline of following Jesus all the way, the choice toward the will of God is always yes. Say yes now, so the decision is already settled. It will set your life on fire.

Way of Holiness

God wants His people to be a holy people—the kind of people who live in the world but don't follow the practices of the world. This is a very difficult challenge for every Christian. How can you live this out?

Once you have made the choice to go on with Jesus all the way, never going back to your Egypt, your heart is ready to follow the chain of making other great decisions for God.

> Once you have made the choice to go on with Jesus all the way, never going back to your Egypt, your heart is ready to follow the chain of making other great decisions for God.

Ask yourself the following questions concerning personal holiness. Take this inventory today so the issue of obedience and right living will be solved for the future:

- Am I going to commit adultery or be faithful to my spouse?

- Am I going to be faithful to my spouse emotionally and mentally or be faithful only physically?

- Am I going to have sex now before I get married or wait until God gives me my perfect mate?

- Am I going to keep surfing the Internet onto sites of the flesh or put someone in my life to provide me with accountability?

- Am I going to read the newspaper or read God's Word?

- Am I going to spend more time watching television or working on my relationship with my family?

- Am I going to ignore my friend's eternal destiny or share God's love and forgiveness with him or her?

- Am I going to keep finding time for everything else but prayer or schedule a time to meet with God on my knees?

- Am I going to keep robbing God financially or begin to honor Him through my local church with at least one-tenth of all He has given to me?

- Am I going to pursue the world or pursue holiness?

These are all choices toward personal holiness. The list could go on for several pages. The choice is made one at a time. Choose personal holiness in your life. Set yourself apart from the world and commit yourself to Jesus. When you make the right choice toward personal holiness, your life will catch on fire.

GOING ON WITH JESUS ALL THE WAY

Does your life need to be set on fire? Do not sit by the campfire warming your hands and watching what Jesus and His people do. Jump in today. God wants to set your life on fire.

Remember: Every choice is a God choice! In each choice you move closer to Jesus or farther away from Him. Where are you right now? Yesterday's embers are not good enough. You need a fresh fire kindling within you so that others will see your life as set ablaze by the Spirit of God. It will all be settled when you make one choice.

Decide today for the rest of your life: "I will not turn back, for I am going on with Jesus all the way!" Become a twenty-first-century Polycarp.

Get ready! When you adopt this spiritual discipline, your life will be ignited by the power of the Holy Spirit of God. Adopting this spiritual discipline will become another deep ember that will set your life ablaze before others.

CHAPTER 4

EARLY, FIRST, OR NOTHING

I have a friend who was raised in Oregon. When he was a child, his family spent their summer vacations in a beach cottage in the town of Neskowin. In his leisure time, he would walk the beach as far as he could see, looking for various things that had washed upon the shore. One of the best treasures of all was finding a perfect sand dollar—one that was free of cracks and chips. But perfect sand dollars were difficult to find.

In his adult years, he returned to that Oregon beach. The first morning of their trip, the sand dollar hunt was on. He and his family searched for sand dollars that had washed up on shore, but their diligent efforts were in vain. This did not discourage them greatly. The next morning, they got up about the same time and continued their search for sand dollars. Again they found nothing.

Although they were starting to get discouraged, they repeated their search on the third day. He saw a woman walking up the beach with a bag full of shells. Many of them were whole sand dollars—just the kind they had been searching for the past three mornings. He asked her where she had found all those sand dollars. She told him that she found them at least one mile from where they were on the beach.

He thought, *We are not going far enough!* He realized that if he continued his quest that day, the sand dollars would already be gone. So he decided that he would not only go farther the next morning, but he would also start much earlier so he could beat everyone else to the beach.

When the alarm went off at 5:30 A.M., some of his family joined him on his persistent search for sand dollars. After walking about three-quarters of a mile down the beach, they had found only a couple of sand dollars. While some returned to the cottage, he and others pressed on toward the prize. They continued to walk farther.

In the next hundred yards, there were at least one dozen sand dollars within a thirty-foot radius. This motivated them, and their walk continued. Could there be more? As they walked farther, they found more perfect sand dollars. In all, they collected more than 125 perfect sand dollars. It was about two miles to this cache of sand dollars, which meant a four-mile round-trip walk in the soft sand. They were tired, so they started back to their seaside cottage.

Since they were so rewarded in their search, they went again early the next morning. In this repeat search, they discovered at least an additional 150 perfect sand dollars. For this trip, the sand dollar treasure hunt was over.

Think about the lessons my friend and his family learned in searching for sand dollars: They wanted treasure, they got up early, they traveled farther, and they exceeded their goals beyond their dreams. This story illustrates a spiritual principle I want you to consider with me.

Before I bring you along on the spiritual discipline we will discuss in this chapter, I want you to know that this is not a *rulebook,* but a *guidebook*. I am not trying to put a guilt trip on you. What is a practice for one person may not be a practice for another. I am trying to motivate and release you in your walk with Christ. At the same time, I am going to call you to go farther than perhaps you have ever been, wherever that may be in relationship to this spiritual discipline.

In this chapter, I want to highlight a principle that leads to the spiritual discipline of a daily time with God. This principle is what I call *the early or first principle*. This principle means that you need to spend time with God early each morning or first in your day.

In all humility, I cannot even remember the last day that I did not practice this principle in my life. For at least twenty-five years, I have either begun my day with God early in the morning or put Him first on the agenda for the day. In the most recent years, my mornings have begun at 4:00 A.M. on Sunday through Thursday. My agenda begins with private time with Jesus. On Friday or Saturday, I sleep later, but the first item on the agenda as soon as I arise is private time with Jesus. Of course, if I am traveling or on vacation, this schedule is forced to change. A breakup in schedule is helpful in all of our lives.

While you are reading this, you may be saying to yourself, "If that is where he is coming from, I cannot and will not do that." Remember: This is not a rulebook, but a guidebook. Let the early or first principle provoke you to go farther than you have ever been. Others might think, *How can I do that when I have a 5:30 A.M. flight?* Use your time in the car on the way to the air-

> Do not turn on the radio immediately and fill your mind with news and sports. Let God have His rightful place—first place in your day, every day.

port to concentrate on God and His greatness, as well as what He might want to choose to do with you through the day. Do not turn on the radio immediately and fill your mind with news and sports. Let God have His rightful place—first place in your day, every day.

WHY YOU NEED TIME WITH JESUS

There is no more important part of my day than the time I spend with God. There is no other appointment that is any more important than meeting with Jesus early or first every day.

I am often asked, "Is your time with God always beneficial to you?" My answer is, "Not at all times." When someone hears me give that answer, I know they are thinking, *Aha! I got him.* Because every day is not a Pentecost in my time with God, they feel that I should not bother to have one at all. Others ask, "Do you feel bound in your life by following the early or first principle?" My answer is, "No, because the principle gives me plenty of freedom, regardless of my schedule for that day." Another question I am asked many times is, "Do you always feel like getting up early?" I quickly reply,

"Absolutely not. I am not a morning person. Yet the spiritual discipline calls me to do it, regardless of how I feel or what my schedule may be for the day."

I really think that no one modeled this principle more than Jesus Himself. He rose early to spend time with His Father in heaven. This is clear throughout the Gospels. If the Son of God felt the need to be with God the Father, where do you think that places you and me?

I believe one of the major reasons you spend time with God is illustrated in the fifteenth chapter of the Gospel of John. Jesus painted a very clear illustration that He is the vine and His disciples are the branches. Just as the vine gives the needed juices and life to the branches so that leaves and fruit can be born, Jesus gives us the power to have productive and fruitful lives. Jesus talked about the importance of cleaving to Him as the vine by telling us that we will not have productive and fruitful lives unless we abide in Him.

The only way to real spiritual productivity and fruitfulness is to abide in Jesus every day. The word *abide* means "to remain in or stay in or continue in." Therefore, we are to remain in Jesus, to stay with Jesus, to continue in Jesus. This means time with Jesus is imperative every day in your life.

For you to see how strong and important this is, read what is recorded in John 15:5. Jesus said, "I am the vine, you are the branches; he who abides in Me and I in him, he bears much fruit, for *apart from Me you can do nothing*" (emphasis added). Jesus said that apart from Him we can do nothing. When He said "nothing," He meant nothing!

He did not mean, "You take care of what you can handle on your own, and when you are in a bind, come talk to Me about it." He did not mean, "Do your best and if it doesn't work out, then come to Me." He did not mean, "Come to Me only when you are in crisis." Jesus did not mean any of these things.

Jesus meant what He said. He meant that there is not one person who is exempt from the imperative need to abide daily in Him. He knew the weakness of human flesh. He was in it. He knew the temptations of the world. He was living in it. He knew there was no way in the world for any of us to make it without staying in, continuing in, and abiding in Him daily.

You need time with Jesus every day so you can have a *productive* life. Surely you desire to live a productive life—a life with purpose and direction. The only way you are ever ensured of having a productive life is to remain in Jesus each day.

You need time with Jesus every day so you can live a *fruitful* life—a life that represents the character of Jesus Christ and operates with the mind of Jesus Christ. A personality seminar will not grant you a fruitful life. Reading another book on leadership or family will not give to you a fruitful life. Attending another Bible study cannot give you a fruitful life. You will only experience a fruitful life when you are spending quality, uninterrupted, and private time with Jesus daily.

You need time with Jesus every day so you can live a *powerful* life. Surely you have lost enough in life already. If you're like me, you have failed God miserably at times. Each one of us has tried and tried until we are tired of trying. We are going at this the wrong way! Abiding in Jesus is the only way we will live a powerful life. This is God's way for you and me. Jesus could not have made it clearer to us when He said, "Apart from Me you can do nothing!" Friend, this is clear enough for me. I am not going against what Jesus said.

You need time with Jesus every day. It is the only way you will live a productive, fruitful, and powerful life. Spending time with Jesus daily is your only prescription for real success in life.

Discard the excuses you tend to fall back on when you tell God and others all the reasons you cannot do it. Jesus was busier than you have ever been in your life, yet He found the time to be with the Father. You can find the time to be with Jesus. The length of one day has not changed since He lived. He had twenty-four hours each day, just like you. There is a way, and your spiritual survival depends on it.

To have a life on fire, you must spend time with God daily. There is no way the fire within is as powerful without time with Jesus. When a person does not have a regular time with God, they need to renew the fire within. The fire within you is ignited when you spend time with God daily. I do not know of a more important spiritual discipline for all Christians than daily time with God.

In my life and ministry, I have listened to many people tell me their failures in the Christian life. Some have been very mature and some very immature in their faith. Yet without exception, whenever I begin to dig deep into their lives, there is always one common denominator: They have neglected to spend time with Jesus. Sometimes we just don't get it! We need to be with Jesus every day.

Christ could not have been any clearer or more passionate about our need to spend time with Him when He said, "Apart from Me you can do nothing." Just take Jesus at His word. If you do, your life will be set on fire in ways that will put you on a spiritual dimension you have never been on before.

My life has been blessed in an extraordinary way. It has little to none to do with giftedness, ability, or appearance. Whenever I am asked, "To what do you contribute your success in life and ministry?", without exception, I always tell them the same thing. I believe God has poured out His blessings on my life in an extraordinary way because of the time I spend with Him. Certainly God's grace even precedes that. However, nothing in my life has helped me more than spending time with Jesus every day.

My goal in this chapter is not to give to you the resources to use during your time with God. My goal is to call you to the treasure of being with Jesus and to challenge you to go farther with Him than you have ever been before. For a specific plan you can use in your time with God, as well as a plan you can customize for your life, see my book *How to Pray*.[1]

In my time with God every day, I talk to God and listen to what He is saying to me. I read God's Word, permitting His Spirit to breathe life to me. In my daily time with God, I confess the sins I have committed. In this time, I also seek the filling of the Holy Spirit in my life. I need His precious Spirit to fill me if I am going to walk victoriously over my own flesh, my own sin, and the devil.

> I need His precious Spirit to fill me if I am going to walk victoriously over my own flesh, my own sin, and the devil.

Abiding in Jesus is about receiving the filling of the Holy Spirit daily—in fact, even momentarily. When you blow it in life, confess your sin and be filled with the Holy Spirit. This is the process of abiding in Jesus while you are walking throughout the day.

The high ground in the Christian life is found in the presence of Jesus Christ. I hope you know the importance of spending time with God daily. So just do it!

BACK TO THE BEACH

Do you remember the lessons that my friend and his family learned in their search for sand dollars? Let's review for a moment: They wanted treasure, they got up earlier, they traveled farther, and they exceeded their goals beyond their wildest dreams. Does this have anything to do with spending time with Jesus? Absolutely!

Treasure

Jesus said, "For where your treasure is, there will your heart be also" (Matt. 6:21). A treasure is something you value in life. Jesus said that whatever you value shows the Father where your heart really is. Words mean little while actions mean everything.

After striking out three days in a row, my friend and his family found their valued treasure, the perfect sand dollar, on the morning of the fourth day. Like many of us, they searched diligently for what they saw as a treasure.

Let me ask you a very personal question: Do you value God

enough to do whatever it takes to meet with Him in your life? Time with God is to be cherished as a treasure in the life of the believer.

Early

My friend learned to do whatever it took to find the treasure of those perfect sand dollars. Remember, the three days they struck out, they headed down the beach at 9:00 A.M. The two days they found the treasure, they started at 5:30 A.M. Since it was necessary for them to start early to discover the treasure, they got up earlier, even on their vacation.

Many of us with complicated and busy lives may have to get up earlier to reach the treasure of being with God daily. The schedule is full enough already. Drive time demands certain things in your schedule. Sometimes that means getting up earlier. Very early drive time demands creativity so you can meet with God while you are driving. Just as my friend had to pay the price of getting up earlier to find the perfect sand dollars, many of you will need to pay the price of getting up earlier to meet with God daily.

Farther

My friend traveled farther up the beach away from his cottage in order to find the perfect sand dollars. He not only had to start earlier, but he had to go farther to discover his treasure.

Sometimes the treasure of a life set on fire involves going farther with Jesus. Make the God choice to go with Jesus all the way. Even if that means farther than you have ever been . . . go for it!

Farther may mean different things to different people. For example, farther to some means just making the decision to meet with God daily. For others, farther may mean deciding to meet God early or first each day. Farther may also mean more time or greater focus or a more private place. The Holy Spirit will personalize it for you. All I know is when I am willing to go farther with Jesus, the treasure is worth it!

Dreams

My friend exceeded his goal of discovering those sand dollars beyond his wildest dreams. On the first, second, and third days, their dreams were shattered. No sand dollars were found in spite of their diligent quest! When they got up earlier and were willing to go farther, their goal was more than reached. Day four—125 sand dollars. Day five—150 sand dollars. Their dreams were met above and beyond what they ever imagined!

We will reach our dreams for God when we are willing to start earlier and to go farther than we ever have gone before. Usually the price of sacrifice determines the value of the treasure. Do you have dreams for your life that have just not been met? Perhaps now they seem impossible. Practice spiritually what my friend practiced practically in his search for sand dollars.

Time with Jesus has far more value than sand dollars. You may be willing to get up earlier and go farther for something in this world. Yet there is nothing more valuable or that will last longer in your life than being with the greatest treasure of all, Jesus Christ.

> . . . there is nothing more valuable or that will last longer in your life than being with the greatest treasure of all, Jesus Christ.

Karen always had big dreams for her life. She was raised in a wonderful Christian home. Her parents were well educated and encouraged her to study diligently. They mentored her spiritually to be a great woman of God.

Karen went to college and fell in love with the study of law. Since her grades were outstanding, she pursued graduate studies. In time, Karen not only achieved her college degree, but her law degree as well.

Out of college, she was hired by a major firm in a large city in the southwest United States. As always, she rose to the top, this time in her career. Soon she became a partner in the firm. Financial prosperity followed her remarkable success at such a young age. Her parents were astounded. Even Karen was astounded. God had been more than good to her.

After three years, Karen began to feel an emptiness. She had dated occasionally, but now she was not even sure she wanted to marry. So the emptiness was not because of a lack of companionship with men. She was a highly successful lawyer, so the emptiness was not because her goals were not being reached.

As was her practice, she went to her parents in this time of need. Within the first hour of their conversation, they diagnosed the cause of Karen's emptiness. Karen's emptiness existed because of a spiritual problem. Karen was active in a church and had made a commitment to be involved in weekly worship and Bible study, but she was not abiding in the Vine. Her life was filled with emptiness in spite of her success. During her high-school years, she had been faithful to spend time with Jesus every day, but she had neglected her daily time with God during college and law school. What happened? She got too busy for Jesus. Sound familiar?

As she shared her busy schedule with her parents, they challenged her to get up earlier and to be willing to go farther with Jesus than she had ever gone before. They told her that the emptiness would soon dissipate if she would treasure her time with God as much as she treasured her career.

God turned Karen's life upside down! Within weeks, she told her parents that the emptiness had disappeared. She had discovered that being with God daily filled the void. When she called home to her parents, their conversation was not simply about what was happening in the law firm; it centered on what God had been doing in her life since she started spending time with Jesus every day.

Just as Karen needed to renew the fire within, do you? It is time for you to want the treasure of being with Jesus so much in your life that you are willing to alter your schedule and desires, if necessary.

PLEADING MY FINAL CASE

The spiritual discipline of spending time with Jesus every day is essential. I have tried to illustrate this truth for you in this chapter by giving you the early or first principle: Get up early to be with Jesus or you place Him first in your day, every day. I know that this is only a guidebook, but I would be remiss if I did not level with you. The secret to a life on fire is early, first, or nothing!

A Case for Early

I mentor a group of my young staff members on a monthly basis. In this two-hour meeting, I teach them various things about life and ministry. As I have the privilege of touching these twenty men monthly, it is my desire to mentor them in the faith.

In one of our meetings, I gave them a biblical case for the importance of a strong work ethic. I laid before them the personal challenges they would have in ministry in regard to a strong work ethic. To help them have this kind of work ethic, I gave them several goals. I closed that session telling them about how they could improve their work ethic.

In that final section, I challenged them to start their day early in the morning. I told them that if they would get up at 5:00 A.M. for thirty days in a row, for only five days per week, they would see their personal productivity as a person and as a minister go up at least 30 to 40 percent. I told them if they accepted this personal challenge, they would never return to beginning their day at a later time. Many of them accepted the challenge and are still practicing it today.

The reason that early morning is so great for your time with God is that it is uninterrupted time. Few people are stirring at 5:00 A.M., so you can have privacy with the Lord. Uninterrupted time with God really goes a long way!

Another reason the early morning is so great for your time with

God is that it is focused time. Your mind is not busy with the demands of job or family in the early hour. Jesus can receive your focus. Your time with God will not be something you do merely to check it off your "To Do" list. Instead, this time can be focused, unrushed, meaningful, and personal—just the way He wanted us to cling to Him.

The early morning to be with God does not have to mean 5:00 A.M. for you. It could mean just getting up thirty minutes before you do right now. Start with twenty minutes earlier. Do whatever it takes to get yourself out of the "rush factor" and into a concentrated, focused, and private time with Jesus.

If you are willing to get up earlier to chase after the sand dollars of this world, surely you are willing to get up earlier to be with Jesus. When you do, your life will be set on fire.

A Case for First

The principle does not live and die on the "early," though meeting God in the early hours of the morning is invaluable. The principle of being with Jesus does hang on the "first" for all of us. Remember, it is early *or* first.

Throughout Scripture, God places value on things that are first. He wants our first love. He wants our first tenth in giving. He wants us to worship with fellow believers on the first day of the week.

We need to seek Jesus first every day—before CNN or SportsCenter, before *USA TODAY* or your local newspaper. Spend time with Jesus before leaving the house, unless your drive time is early or you have a flight time that is unusually early. If so, adjust and spend time with Him privately in the car, even before you listen to music. Remember, we are trying to let God build deep, burning embers in our lives, not to give us quick burns that attempt to be a substitute for the real person of Jesus.

Seeking Jesus first today and every day will bring order to your day and provide the balance that is so hard to achieve in this busy world. He is the Vine, not a Bible study, a Christian praise song, or a new CD. He is your source for living. There is not one person or experience that can be the Vine but Jesus Christ.

> He is the Vine, not a Bible study, a Christian praise song, or a new CD. He is your source for living. There is not one person or experience that can be the Vine but Jesus Christ.

Only He can set your life on fire. Being with Him first every day will ignite your life like nothing else. All other spiritual disciplines hinge on the success of the early or first principle of being with Jesus every day.

A Case for Nothing

Why do I need to make a case for nothing? Because the truth of the matter is this: It is early, first, or nothing in your life! If you do not spend time with Jesus early each day or at the first of each day, your life will be nothing! That is exactly what Jesus said in John 15:5: "Apart from Me you can do nothing." "Nothing" means *nothing*.

Your future is bleak without time with Jesus. Your treasure is vain without time with Jesus. Your personal value is limited without time with Jesus. Your productivity is minimal without time with Jesus. Your life is fruitless without time with Jesus. Your life is powerless without time with Jesus.

Why choose nothing when you can have a life full of spiritual treasure?

I want to challenge you to spend time every day with Jesus. It really is early, first, or nothing. Nothing will set your life on fire more than this spiritual discipline of spending private time with Jesus every day.

CHAPTER 5

LIVING FROM THE INSIDE OUT

How would you like to be the cupbearer to the king? Sounds like royalty, doesn't it? Think about it for a moment. The cupbearer to the king is responsible for serving wine at the king's table and protecting the king from poisoning. Whatever the king drinks, the cupbearer drinks first in case someone is trying to poison the king. Now that is the downside to this job. The upside of the job is that the cupbearer is ranked high in the kingdom and is taken into confidence by the king.

Nehemiah was the highly esteemed cupbearer for Artaxerxes. He was an exiled Jew who had risen to the top of the kingdom of Persia. One day, men came from the city of Jerusalem to give a report to Nehemiah about his homeland. They shared with him that the conditions in Jerusalem were deplorable. The wall around the city was broken down, and the gates were burned with fire. Since the wall was broken down, the city of Jerusalem was vulnerable to all of its enemies, especially since the gates were burned and destroyed.

When Nehemiah heard these words about Jerusalem, he began to weep. For days, his heart was grieved over the devastating news. Nehemiah was so overcome with sorrow that he began to fast and pray before the Lord about the city of Jerusalem. This man not only had a passion for Jerusalem, but he had a great passion for God.

As Nehemiah interceded for his homeland before God, he confessed the sins of the people. He confessed their wickedness and their disobedience to God's commandments. He knew the people of Jerusalem had sinned. He understood that God had brought judgment to Jerusalem. He appealed to God to have mercy upon His people in Jerusalem.

The next time Nehemiah served the king his wine, the king asked him why he looked so sad. Nehemiah reported to the king the conditions that existed in Jerusalem. The king said to him, "Do you have a request?" Nehemiah quickly prayed to the Lord and then requested that the king let him return to Jerusalem to rebuild the wall around the city. The king had such great confidence in Nehemiah that he granted his request. Nehemiah was on his way to Jerusalem.

The project before him was massive, but Nehemiah had confidence in God and in His people to rebuild the wall. At first, Nehemiah's arrival was met with skepticism. Then he took men around the city to share with them his vision of rebuilding the wall. The people caught Nehemiah's vision, and in just days the project began.

The story of the wall being rebuilt around Jerusalem is an amazing account of God's power. Nehemiah's leadership skills were excellent, even though he faced incredible opposition. As his opponents mocked, ridiculed, and tried to destroy what God was doing, Nehemiah stayed focused on what God was doing with the people. In just fifty-two days, the people accomplished the goal of rebuilding the wall around the city.

Hope had been restored to Jerusalem. This special city of God now enjoyed protection and security. All of this occurred because of one person who lived from the inside out. Do you know what it means to live from the inside out?

Rethink the story with me for a moment. When he heard about the devastation of Jerusalem, Nehemiah did not take matters into his own hands. He did not immediately tell the king, "I have to go back to Jerusalem." He did not appoint a committee to study the situation in Jerusalem. He did not panic. He did not get angry. He did not overreact. He did not get ahead of God.

How many times do you overreact when you hear bad news? How many times do you take matters into your own hands? How many times do you attempt to organize matters to take care of the problem? How many times do you rush to such a point that you get ahead of God? I am sure we have all been guilty of responding in such a way.

But notice that Nehemiah lived from the inside out. When he heard the news, he went to God in prayer immediately. In the midst of his brokenness, he pursued the God of heaven. He even spent days in fasting and prayer, interceding for his people and the city of Jerusalem.

After he spent time with God, his heart was ready to be used of God. He let the Lord guide the way. The necessary events unfolded before his eyes. The king asked him what he wanted to do—a miracle. The king let him go back to Jerusalem—another miracle. Nehemiah led the people of God to the task—yet another miracle. The people completed the project in fifty-two days in spite of great opposition—the miracle of all miracles! Nehemiah is our example of living from the inside out.

Do you ever respond in this manner when bad news comes into your life? Have you ever taken this type of action when you know something must be done? Do you pray before you fret? Do you pray about the situation and the people before you react? Do you fast and pray over desperate situations in your life? Do you really long to see God work in your life as He did in Nehemiah's life? All of this is possible when you live from the inside out.

> Do you pray before you fret? Do you pray about the situation and the people before you react? Do you fast and pray over desperate situations in your life?

REMEMBER THESE WORDS

One of the great spiritual disciplines in the Christian life is living from the inside out. If you are tired of always trying to get things done in your own power, then embrace the discipline of living from the inside out. If you are physically weary from trying to make things happen, then embrace living from the inside out. If you are disappointed in yourself for overreacting in various situations, then begin to live from the inside out. If you are ready for a fresh wind of God's Spirit in your life, then read on, and I will show you how to live from the inside out.

I want you to remember these very important words about living from the inside out: *What goes on within you will determine what goes on around you. And what goes on within you will determine what goes on through you.* You will never be any greater than your own personal walk with Jesus Christ. You will never see God do anything more through you than what you know He is doing in you. What God does in you will determine what He does in you and around you.

You will never see changes in your outward conduct until you begin to live from the inside out. You will never see changes in the way you respond to others until you begin to live from the inside out. You will never see great spiritual events happening through your life until you see God do some great spiritual things within you. It is called living from the inside out.

You have tried everything else; now try living from the inside out. You have tried several "quick burns," such as conferences, seminars, tapes, books, and music. Try living from the inside out. This is not a quick burn! It is not something that will puff up for a moment to make you think you are on fire, but in reality nothing has changed.

Living from the inside out is a spiritual discipline that will set your life on fire. It will provide the spiritual balance you may need in your life. If you practice what I am going to share with you about this spiritual discipline, you will see great things happen in your spiritual life.

CONVICTIONS

I have some real convictions about what will take place in your life when you begin to live from the inside out. These convictions must be transferred from my heart into your life. In fact, these convictions need to go beyond that. They must grip you and control you. I heard someone say years ago, "A conviction is not something that you have; a conviction is something that has you."

I want to challenge you to embrace the following convictions because they are necessary for you to live from the inside out.

Your Spiritual Walk Will Be Expressed Through Your Priorities

When you truly walk before the Lord with great passion and biblical conviction, your priorities will reflect it. In other words, as your spiritual life goes, so goes the rest of your life. This includes your priorities. When Jesus Christ is really important to you and you are walking with Him daily, your priorities will reflect the importance of that relationship. This is living from the inside out.

If you do not have great zeal for the Lord when you sit down and make priorities for your life, your priorities will be wrong. If they happen to be right because you might know the right things to do, you still will not live by them because the fire of God is not burning in your heart. You cannot live outwardly what is not happening inwardly.

If your life seems to be falling apart and you feel disconnected, it is because you have neglected your walk with Christ. Your problem is a spiritual problem. When things are in disarray and you are fretting over the matters at hand, it is because you are not living from the inside out.

Your priorities and your walk with Christ always harmonize. As your walk with Christ goes, so go your priorities. Your walk with Christ will be expressed through your priorities.

Be a Person of Priority

As a Christian, you must determine your priorities and follow them. Your life will flow out of your priorities. Priorities indicate order and rank. Some things in life are more important than others. Under God, you have to determine which of these should become priorities in your life.

Life pulls on you all the time. If you have children, family responsibilities will pull on you. Being a working parent increases the pull. If you are an owner of your own company or a leader in someone else's company, the pull becomes even greater. The more responsibilities you have, the greater your tension.

Let me go one step farther. The more you desire to walk with the Lord, the greater the pressure will become. Now do not get me wrong. Walking with the Lord is your only hope to pull your frazzled and busy life together. However, if you do not have a renewed heart, your desire for the Lord may just tighten the tension. Your hope is to live from the inside out where your walk will be expressed through your priorities.

Overall, the important thing for you to determine in the next few minutes is your need to be a person of priority. Decide that you are no longer going to be ruled by the greatest crisis in your life. Becoming a person of priority is essential for a great spiritual life, as well as an orderly and balanced life. Pursue living from the inside out.

Do Not Live by Your Passions, but by Your Priorities

You are probably somewhat of a passionate person to have purchased this book. The title itself calls you to action. Only a person with inner passion would ever pursue taking action in his or her spiritual life.

I want to make an observation and provide a warning to you. I have observed through the years that people will find a way to accomplish whatever they are pas-

> What people are passionate about, they will find a way to do.

sionate about. If you are passionate about your job, it will get done. If you are passionate about providing a home-cooked meal daily, you will find a way to make it happen. If you are passionate about spending time with your children, you will make the time to do it. If you are passionate about golf or tennis, it will happen in your life. What people are passionate about, they will find a way to do.

The major warning I want to give to you about this is that many times the things you are passionate about should not be done in the priority you are doing them. This is why a wife is frustrated with her husband when he does not have time to spend with the family but always finds time to play golf with his friends. Is there anything wrong with spending time with the family? No! Is there anything wrong with playing golf? No! What is the problem?

The problem is that her husband is living by his passion, not by his priorities. Remember, a person will always fulfill what he or she is most passionate about in life. What needs to happen in this husband's life is for him to re-evaluate his priorities and live by them. He would tell you before the re-evaluation period that his family was more important to him than his golf game. The only problem is that his life does not show it. The problem is that his priorities are not right.

Do not live by your passion alone, but live by your priorities. When you do this, you will accomplish the things in your life you need and want to accomplish. The result will be balance and order in your life and in the lives of the people around you. This is living from the inside out.

These three convictions need to "have you" in your life, not just "you have them." Living from the inside out is expressing your walk with Christ through your priorities. Living from the inside out is becoming a person of priorities. Living from the inside out is living by your priorities, not merely by your passion.

ISSUES

When you live from the inside out, you will continually encounter several issues. I want to highlight some of these issues so you will be alert to what will contest this lifestyle and compete with what I know God wants to do in you as you live from the inside out.

Change

The only constant thing in life is change. The world population is exploding. The technological boom is beyond all of our imaginations as we now live in a world with e-mail and e-commerce. Now the world is at our fingertips. Things we have never thought of happening are now taking place.

A few months ago, our church began to broadcast our Sunday morning services live, via the Internet. We are receiving responses from all over the world. Thousands of people are now worshiping with us each week over the Internet. Amazing!

We recently sent a mission team to Taipei, Taiwan. While they were eight thousand miles away from home, I carried on a conversation with them over the Internet through instant messaging. Years ago, we would have no means of communication with our mission teams without it costing major dollars. Things have changed, and they will continue to change. The challenge is to keep up with the changes.

With the constant changes in family, schedule, communication, and business, you are under immense pressure in your life. You may not realize it, but you are under great pressure.

When you determine to live from the inside out, you will be much better equipped to handle change in your life. You will not let it get out of balance, nor will you alter your life every time something new happens. Be prepared for change, and handle it God's way by living from the inside out.

Future

The future seemed questionable during the days prior to our transition into the twenty-first century. Y2K alarmists had raised multiple questions in the minds of millions. It seemed that the world was living for the new millennium. What would the twenty-first century be like?

I do not know the answer to that question, but I do know that the future is critical. What happens during the next few years will determine many things about each of our lives.

What I do know is that when you live from the inside out, the future is your friend, not your enemy. The word *dread* is not in your vocabulary; instead, you are excited about the opportunities before you. You have confidence in God that translates into great faith. Using the future for your own advantage and goals becomes secondary to using them for the Lord. The future is for God's purposes, not for our own. This is what it means to live from the inside out.

Time

Time seems to be minimizing in each of our lives. The common excuse people give you about most anything is either, "I am too busy" or, "I do not have enough time." Both of these statements represent the fact that we have some enormous issues in relationship to time. I just do not think that this type of conduct honors God.

There has to be more to life than running around like a chicken with its head cut off. Have you ever witnessed that process? I used to watch it at my grandmother's house. Once beheaded, the chicken's body would run around in disarray before its death.

This is how most people live in today's world. They are running around from crisis to crisis with their lives in disarray! The real tragedy is that many have gotten so used to this frantic pace of life that it is accepted as the norm for our day. Not true!

We have as much time today as we have ever had. Each week, you are blessed with 168 hours. The issue is not time. You have time. The issue is the way you use your time—in other words, your priorities. When you live from the inside out, you will have more time in your life. Guaranteed!

Satan

Satan is your only enemy. Change, future, and time are issues, but Satan is your enemy.

In John 10:10, Jesus taught that Satan comes to steal, kill, and destroy. When he plays the game of life with us, he plays for keeps. He always lures you away from God. He is like a rattlesnake that you permit to cuddle up next to you through the secret sins of your life. In time, he will strike you and kill you. Satan wants to destroy your family. He wants to destroy your church. He wants to destroy the work of God across the world. He wants to destroy you.

Sounds serious, doesn't it? It is very serious in relationship to your priorities. When you live from the inside out, you will understand that Satan will wage against you and will be at the point of your personal priorities every day, all day. Be ready. You are in a war—a spiritual war with Satan. He will attack you at the point

> When you live from the inside out, you will understand that Satan will wage against you and will be at the point of your personal priorities every day, all day.

of your priorities. He will cause tension at each ranking priority, attempting to stir them up and getting you emotionally distraught. He knows this will defeat you spiritually. The attack will be every day, all day. Count on it! Be ready for it.

The good news is that if you can win the battle of your priorities, you can live from the inside out. If you can win the battle of your priorities, God will make you a great influencer among others because your life will be remarkably different from theirs. Others will be attracted to you because they see something in you they desire to happen within themselves. Become a prioritized person, and you will defeat Satan by becoming an influencer for Christ.

Conversely, if you do not win the battle of your personal priorities, you will not live a consistent, mature, balanced, and spiritually empowered life. Your priorities determine your consistency. Your priorities determine your maturity. Your priorities determine your balance. Your priorities determine your spiritual power. Remember this: Your walk with Christ is demonstrated through your priorities. As your spiritual life goes, so go your priorities. Therefore, so goes the rest of your life.

Living from the inside out will ignite your life with new fire and new power. Do it today, and your priorities will reflect your walk with Jesus Christ.

PRIORITIES

As I emphasize the importance of setting personal priorities, I would be negligent if I did not share with you my own priorities. The following story is an example of how I have learned to live from the inside out.

I am the pastor of a very fast-growing congregation. I have seen our church grow from four thousand members to twelve thousand members. We have a national television ministry. We have a Christian school with just fewer than one thousand students. Our staff has become very large in order to take care of these massive and ever-changing ministries.

All of this has happened while I have walked with my wife, Jeana, through cancer, surgery, and aggressive treatments. Thank God, we have seen Him heal her. I have also been an active part of the lives of my two sons, Josh and Nick. Josh is a student at Ouachita Baptist University, and Nick attends our church's private high school. They are very active in the ministry of our church and are running at a rapid pace like most teenagers and college students in our society.

In addition to all of this, I have served in several positions of leadership within my denomination and outside of my denomination. I am involved in speaking with several ministries around the country. I am always open to what I can do to assist in expanding the kingdom of God.

Why all of these details? Because I would have never survived the incredible transition in family, ministry, and personally without living from the inside out. Without being a prioritized man, I would not be able to accomplish what I am expected to accomplish.

Reports about me would probably be as varied as they are about you. However, the vast majority of people who know me would attest to you that I am a focused and prioritized man who lives from the inside out. As a result, I am happily married to Jeana, both of my boys are very committed to Jesus, and our church is in the greatest year of growth in our history.

Why has this happened? Obviously through the grace of God, but I have also learned that when my fire for God is burning, my spiritual life will be evidenced through the priorities in my life. This is living from the inside out.

I want to share with you my priorities. I have worked through them and believe them to be very biblical. Maybe you sense your priorities need to be different from these, but I am quite convinced that our priorities, when lined up with Scripture, need to all be the same. Let God speak to you about your priorities today.

Priority #1: Your Personal Relationship with God

Nothing is more important than your relationship with God—not your spouse, your children, your church, your job, or your hobbies. Nothing!

> Nothing is more important than your relationship with God—not your spouse, your children, your church, your job, or your hobbies. Nothing!

I have already stated the importance of the early or first principle in your spiritual time with God daily. You need to meet Him early or first every day of your life. This is essential so you can experience balance and order in your life and in the day you are about to encounter. If you do not start right, you will not finish right.

Every other priority is hinged on the success of this priority. Set this priority in concrete or your life will forever be nothing more than shifting sand or quicksand. The only way you will rise above is to walk with God above it. This is the heart of living from the inside out.

Priority #2: Your Family

In the mid-eighties, I determined that my ministry was not worth losing my family. I determined never to sacrifice my wife or children on the altar of ministry success. No job is worth losing your family. Do not sacrifice your marriage and children on the altar of your career success. Under God, it is not right.

I am convinced that families are falling apart all over America, both inside and outside of the church, because of a lack of personal priorities. When a family lives in crisis, the disorder impacts everyone in the family. When there is little emphasis on the value of each family member's personal faith and walk with Christ, the family will be fragmented, living on the ragged edge.

There is no dress rehearsal for marriage. Every day should mean something to you and your spouse. There is no dress rehearsal for parenting. You have one shot with your children. What are you putting into their lives? They will watch how you live, rather than hear what you say. Be a prioritized person with a prioritized family. God is not the author of confusion.

Make time for your spouse. Jeana and I spend each Friday together. This is our day off together since Sunday is a workday for me. We always have lunch together and hang out with each other. Neither of us breaks this covenant unless we both agree. We are a priority to one another.

Make time for your children. I have canceled speaking engagements to attend various functions for my children. What is important to them should be important to me. Invest time in your children.

Priority #3: Your Church

The Lord has given the church the commission to take the gospel to the world and to teach people in their faith. The church is the center of God's activity in the universe.

Since Jesus died for the church, it should be very important to me. What is important to God should be important to me.

The church should be the center of your life. It should be the people who provide you with loving and caring relationships, the people who hunger to grow in the Lord with you, the people who pray for you, and the people who partner with you to take the gospel of Jesus Christ to your region, to our country, and to the world.

Priority #4: Your Job

Christians should model a strong work ethic. You should strive to give your employer an excellent work standard. You should be the type of person who models a balanced life and excels in the workplace.

Your job is what God has given to you to *do*. But God expects you to accomplish something much bigger than your job, something much bigger than you can do alone. What is that? To walk with Jesus with a renewed heart and to meet all the needs of your family. He has provided you income from your job as a resource for you to help take the gospel to the world through your local church. Each one of these things is bigger than you or your job.

When your job takes away from the priorities that are higher in rank, you have a priority problem. Yes, you *might* have a job problem, but the problem is more likely that you need to get hold of your life. You need to let God empower you with His priorities.

Priority #5: Your Recreation

God says we need to be re-created on a weekly basis. This is why He has given us a day of rest. The tragedy is that many think this day of rest belongs to them and their recreation. You are wrong! Look back at the list of priorities we have covered so far. This is number five, at the bottom of the totem pole.

Recreation is important, but it also has a place. I decided years ago that I wanted to be a better dad than golfer. I am glad to let you know that my boys and my golf game demonstrate that I met that goal.

Keep your recreation in the order of your priorities. When it takes away from your walk with God, it is wrong. If you can find time to enjoy recreation but do not have a time with God daily, you have a priority problem. Do not let your recreation take you away from your family. They need you more than you need recreation. Learn to do things the whole family enjoys doing. Do not let your recreation take away from your church. When you are running your children to soccer tournaments on Sunday or teeing off on the green rather than growing with your family in church, you are making a terrible mistake you will pay for the rest of your life. It is just not right. When you let your recreation take away from your job in any way, you are going to lose not only your testimony in the workplace, but also the respect of your fellow workers.

When you live for recreation or anything else other than the Lord, you are in a very vulnerable time in your life. You need to get a grip and let God set your life on fire.

Remember, you will win or lose your battle with Satan at the point of your priorities. You may have given some ground to him in this area. Your life and family will eventually show it. Take back the land! Get your priorities right.

THE DECISIONS ARE MADE, EVEN THE HARD ONES

When your personal priorities are not in line, your life will be disorderly and ineffective, resulting in much indecision. Nothing creates disorder or makes you more ineffective than misplaced priorities or no priorities. The result will be that you either struggle with indecision or make wrong decisions. Both are very costly.

When you establish biblical priorities, the decisions in your life are already made, even the hard ones. From the details of unimportant decisions to the challenges of big decisions, you only have one thing to do: Look at the order of your biblical priorities. They will determine whether you have a time with God, a love for your spouse and children, a zeal for the church, and a desire to achieve on the job.

> From the details of unimportant decisions to the challenges of big decisions, you only have one thing to do: Look at the order of your biblical priorities.

God did not make life to be complicated. Our sin of failing to set biblical priorities has complicated life. God is the creator of order, balance, and effectiveness. We should follow His lead. Nehemiah did, and look what he accomplished with his life.

Living from the inside out is exciting, balanced, and a testimony to others. When you choose to live from the inside out, you are making a choice to set your life on fire.

CHAPTER 6

RESCUING GOD

There are myriad views about God in American Christianity. These various views are sending unclear signals about who God really is to a world without Jesus Christ. Let's take a brief look at the landscape of American Christianity.

One view of God holds that if you pray hard enough, God will heal you. It does not matter what disease you have, God will heal you if you are praying in the right manner. It is true that your faith influences how effective your prayer really is, but people having this view believe if you pray with enough faith, you will be healed from any disease. They say if you have enough faith, nothing bad will happen to you. It does not matter what your problem is—sickness, employment needs, financial struggles, family problems, or a lack of vision—their answer to everything is that you have to have more faith.

Consider how the world views that perspective of God. They have seen Christians pray for other Christians who have died. They have heard that even the people who have promoted that view of God have died. They scratch their heads, wondering if the people are strange or God is strange. They are not sure, so they stay away from God and Christians.

When people in the unchurched community go through hard times, they are not even drawn to the church because they think all churches practice this spiritual exercise. They do not have faith in God; therefore, our God would have nothing to say to them through their hard times. They do not talk to the Christians they know because they think they would receive the same answer they hear over television and the radio: "Just have more faith."

Another view of God that is very popular is that if you give enough money to various ministries, you will be wealthy. The people who preach an ideology of wealth attempt to sport that look before their followers. They claim that the reason people are poor is that they have never given in order to get wealthy. I saw a pastor recently ask his congregation to stand if they believed God that they would make one million dollars this year. The entire congregation stood, except for a few. This preacher, like many others, really believes that God wants everyone to be prosperous with beautiful clothing, expensive cars, big houses, and expensive jewelry. These preachers challenge their listeners to give "seed gifts" to their ministries so God will begin their cycles of prosperity.

The non-Christian population of America is turned away by that view, rather than drawn to it. They may know Christians who are kind, gentle, and caring but do not have great sums of money. The "wealth" philosophy of God appears to them as nonsense. This view of God will not fly in the Third World countries around the globe. Even people without Christ realize that God is not a supreme being who pours out wealth to people just because they give to someone's ministry.

Another view of God propagates that when you disobey God as a Christian, God will judge you in a harsh manner. He is an angry Father in heaven who will knock you back into line the moment you choose to disobey Him. Therefore, the motivation to serve God, by many who believe this view, is a dreaded fear of God.

When non-Christians hear that view of God, why would they want to have God in their lives? They know they are not perfect. Therefore, if God is going to punish them severely every time they do something wrong, they want nothing to do with Him.

Evaluate the view of God that says praise is the answer to everything in your life. If you will continually say, "Praise the Lord," all matters in your life will work out. Therefore, constantly say those words and always have your praise music on so you will be able to have everything work out all right.

Think about a lost woman who has a friend who holds this view of God. Her friend is constantly saying, "Praise the Lord!" Then her friend gets the call that her son was killed in a car accident. She sees her friend walk through the devastation and the loss. She thinks, *What happened to all the praise?* She shakes her head with sympathy for her Christian friend but bewilderment with her God.

An observation I have made through the years about people whose ministries promote any one of these false views of God is that I have never seen any of them completely committed to seeing people around the world come to faith in Jesus Christ. They are not Great Commission Christians. They are so caught up in their improper views that a traumatic imbalance has happened to them and their ministries. A person's view of the Great Commission will always tell you where they are in their theological perspective.

I want to make something very clear about the aforementioned false views of God and those who hold them. I am sure that many people who hold these views have a great faith in Jesus Christ. I am confident that many of them truly desire to help people. Yet their biblical imbalance has led many people down the path of a counterfeit view of God.

In addition, I want you to understand that I believe when we pray, people can be healed. If they are followers of Jesus and die, they will ultimately be healed. I also believe that when you give, God blesses you in your life. The Word of God promises that your needs will be met, but it does not say that you will necessarily become wealthy.

I do believe in the power of faith, but I believe more in the power of God. God will place me in the fire periodically to build my faith. My faith will not keep me from problems, but it sees me through my problems. I believe that if I disobey God, He will judge me. Yet, He will do so to guide me to Him with love, not out of severe discipline of me, unless I have sinned willfully and greatly.

> God will place me in the fire periodically to build my faith. My faith will not keep me from problems, but it sees me through my problems.

I also believe in the power of praise. However, I do not believe that praise means that everything in your life will work out. I believe that God uses all kinds of things that happen to us for our own good. Praise has a definite part in our spiritual lives, but will not prevent trouble from occurring in my life.

FANNING THE FIRE

I have already discussed the importance of implementing specific spiritual disciplines that will set your life on fire. Now I am going to share several spiritual disciplines that will fan the fire in your life. Just as oxygen is essential for an effective fire, these disciplines will fan the fire that God has set in your life.

LEAD THE CHARGE

I want to ask you to lead the charge in rescuing God. Do not misunderstand me—I know God does not need to be rescued from anything. He is a very big God and has the power to take care of Himself.

I want to ask you to lead the charge in rescuing God and His character from the low view that many people have of Him in American Christianity. People in our country cannot see the One true God for who He is because of all the colored glasses we have put on people toward spiritual things. When they think of God, they are trying to see Him through these distorted views. They are having a very difficult time getting a clear view of who God really is.

I am appealing to you to recognize the importance of having a high view of God. Not one that attempts to drag Him down to our level, but one that is proper and right according to Holy Scripture. We need to join together to rescue others from a low or an unclear view of God. This will rescue the great God of heaven and His true character from being minimized by the inaccurate views that people hold of Him. This is what I mean by rescuing God.

The reason our view of God is so important is that it will determine the way we live. If we want to see the fire within renewed continually by us fanning the fire, then a proper view of God is essential.

WHAT AN IMPROPER VIEW OF GOD WILL DO

Simon practiced magic in Samaria. When he was in his dark world of magic, he astounded people with what he could do. The people declared that he had the great power of God. Obviously, they had a very distorted view of God.

When Simon heard the good news that Philip was preaching, he believed. The Scripture says he also was baptized. As he walked with Philip in those days, he was amazed at the miracles and signs taking place.

When the saints in Jerusalem learned that Samaria was receiving the gospel message, they sent Peter and John there. They came to lead the people to the power of the Holy Spirit in their lives. When Simon saw them laying hands on the people and the people receiving the Holy Spirit, he offered them money. He attempted to bribe them for the Holy Spirit.

The eighth chapter of the Book of Acts records this story: "But Peter said to him, 'May your silver perish with you, because you thought you could obtain the gift of God with money! You have no part or portion in this matter, for your heart is not right before God'" (vv. 20–21). They went on to tell him to repent of the wickedness in his heart. Simon asked them to pray to God on his behalf so that nothing of what they said would come upon him.

What was Simon's problem? His problem was an improper view of God. He may or may not have truly believed (I will leave that up to God), but he should have checked all of his magical baggage at the door. He would perform magical acts with money and some said he had the power of God. I guess he thought that money would give to him what Peter and John were praying for the people to receive. Peter was indignant toward Simon because of his low view of God. Peter told him that God was not motivated by his money! Simon's heart was not right because his view of God was distorted.

Some of you may have been raised with a poor or low view of God. Some of you may have been mentored while you were young in the faith by someone who taught you a poor view of God. Do what Simon failed to do. Check all of your baggage at the door! Start over with God. See Him as He really is.

> Check all of your baggage at the door! Start over with God. See Him as He really is.

If you do not have a proper view of God, let me share where that will lead you in life.

Quench the Fire, Rather than Fan It

An improper view of God will quench the fire in your life. Simon quenched what God was doing in Samaria with his low view of God. It is important that you see what will happen in your life if you maintain an improper view of God. The fire will be quenched, rather than fanned.

I have seen this happen numerous times in our church's worship. God's presence is powerful and reigning in our midst. The moment is one of solitude. The Holy Spirit is using a vocalist to grip our hearts with the powerful message of a song. As soon as the soloist concludes, someone begins to clap with great insensitivity, forgetting that God, not a person, is to get the glory. I am not against some applause in worship, but there is a time and place for everything. People who demonstrate that kind of insensitivity do so because they think that all praise has to be hyped because the God in their minds would want that.

When this type of thing occurs, the fire is quenched. A great moment that God has created becomes the brunt of human insensitivity. Once my heart was in worship before the Father, but now it is grieved by human response.

When you view God improperly, you will quench the fire within you, rather than fanning it.

Promote a Counterfeit Fire

An improper view of God will also promote a counterfeit fire, rather than fanning the real fire. If Simon's request had been made in the twenty-first-century American church, some would have taken him up on his offer. They would have said, "Just place your money here. Now we will pray for you." They might have squinted their eyes, raised their voices, and promised an amazing result to Simon, all because their God is for sale.

Simon would have left, talking about what happened to him. He would have shared it with others and invited them to get what he had. Little would he have known that he had counterfeit fire. Just a quick burn! His improper view of God would have promoted a counterfeit fire, rather than fanning the real fire.

I am convinced that Peter rebuked Simon so quickly because he recognized the request as counterfeit. He did not want to confuse the people over the real fire and counterfeit fire. Oh, that spiritual leaders in America had that kind of boldness today.

The reason a lot of people think they have something but in reality do not is because of a low view of God. All they have is counterfeit fire. Only a right and proper view of God will fan the true fire. All else will quench it or attempt to give you something that is not real.

A PROPER VIEW OF GOD

I want to lift the spiritual discipline that I am highlighting in this chapter from the foundation I have laid in the previous paragraphs of this chapter. This spiritual discipline will fan the fire in your life that will result in your being a Great Commission Christian.

The spiritual discipline of rescuing God will help you keep a proper view of God. This will lead you to sharing Him with those who do not know Jesus Christ as their personal Savior and Lord. This discipline will ignite the fire in your life. Few things will fan the fire in your life like sharing the good news of Jesus Christ.

I am convinced the reason most Christians are not aggressively sharing their faith in Jesus Christ with persons who do not know Him is because their view of God is very weak. They do not see Him as a loving God who is in the spiritual business of reconciling the lost world unto Himself. This is why Jesus Christ died on the cross for the forgiveness of our sins: He died to reconcile us to God.

When we see God like this, we will share Christ with those who do not know Him personally. When we share Him, regardless of the response we receive, we will see the fire fanned within our lives.

Betsie and Corrie ten Boom understood the power of this spiritual discipline. On the first evening in the concentration camp in Ravensbruck, they began their journey in this discipline. The place was filthy and dark. The bedding was soiled and rancid. There were more people than bedding, so space was very crowded.

Corrie began to feel sharp stabs of pain all over her legs. She bolted upright, striking her head on the bunk as she did—only to discover that the place was crawling with fleas.

Betsie thought for a moment and said, "He's given us the answer . . . in the Bible this morning. Where was it?"

Corrie fumbled for her Bible, making sure the guard did not see it. Corrie knew it was in 1 Thessalonians. She began to read, "'Comfort the frightened, help the weak, be patient with everyone. See that none of you repays evil for evil, but always seek to do good to one another and to all.'" It seemed that the words were written just for them in the Ravensbruck concentration camp. Corrie continued to read, "'Rejoice always, pray constantly, give thanks in all circumstances.'"

Betsie said, "That is what we can do, Corrie. We can give thanks to God." They began to give thanks to God for their lives and the opportunity that God was giving them to touch the lives of the people in Ravensbruck. They knew God wanted to use them to impact the lives of others.

Corrie and Betsie's view of God was proper, healthy, and right! They knew God was in control of all things, even the events at Ravensbruck. They knew that God loved everyone, even the Germans. They knew God wanted to use them to share His love and message with the people of Ravensbruck. All of this happened because of a healthy view of God. The fire in their lives was fanned to burn ablaze because of their desire to impact others with the message of God. This is what kept them going while in Ravensbruck.[1]

I want to urge you to implement the spiritual discipline of rescuing God by having a proper view of Him that will result in a great desire to share Jesus Christ with those who do not know Him personally as Savior and Lord. Yes, it will fan your fire!

When You See God As He Really Is

Saul was a very aggressive leader in the days of the new church of Jesus Christ. He hated Christians with a passion. In fact, he made a practice of killing Christians! The first martyr in the church was Stephen. Saul stood by approvingly when Stephen was stoned to death. Then Saul began his aggressive attack, going house to house arresting Christians, leading them to their eventual doom.

But things changed in Saul's life. One day while he was on his way to Damascus, a great light came down from heaven upon him. Jesus spoke to him and asked him why he was persecuting Jesus! That's right. Saul was not only persecuting His people, but Jesus Himself. Acts 9 records this story in full, but it is interesting to note that Saul was indicted for coming against Jesus. It was as if Jesus said, "Do you not know who are you persecuting? I am Jesus Christ, the Lord!"

On that day, Saul's life changed forever. In time he understood what had happened to him. Jesus Christ had come into his life and transformed him. He turned from killing Christians to being a Christian through a miraculous expression of God's grace in his life. Saul met Jesus Christ as his personal Savior and Lord. His life would never be the same again.

On that day, Saul saw Jesus Christ. Not a counterfeit view of Him, but the real thing! Can you imagine the response of the people when they heard that Saul had become a true follower of Jesus?

Saul's name was later changed to Paul, and he gave the rest of his life to sharing Jesus Christ with everyone who did not know Him as Savior and Lord. He did not go and tell people that he saw Jesus, so "give to my ministry." He did not go and tell people that he saw Jesus, and "He wants to heal all of you from your physical diseases." He did not go and tell people he saw Jesus, and "He wants you all to be wealthy." No. He told people they needed to have a personal relationship with Jesus Christ as their Savior and Lord. This is what will happen to every Christian when we see God for who He really is.

Available to God

When Saul saw the Lord, he became available to God. When Moses saw the Lord, he became available to God. When the prophet Isaiah saw the Lord, he became available to God. When the disciples saw the resurrected Jesus Christ, they became available to God. When John saw the glorified Jesus Christ, he became available to God.

When you see God as He really is, you will also become available to God. You will not play "hide-and-seek" from God. You will become available to Him. You will not run from God. You will become available to Him. You will not make excuses to God. You will become available to Him. You will not be ashamed to share Christ. You will become available to share Him.

> When you see God as He really is, you will also become available to God. You will not play "hide-and-seek" from God.

Are you available to God today? Are you willing to do whatever

God wants you to do? Our attitude before God needs to be "whenever, wherever, and whatever." This will be our attitude when we see God for who He really is.

God is not so small you can run from Him. God is not so dumb you can make excuses to Him. God is not so weak that you do not need Him. He is God. You are human. Heaven dictates to us, not us to heaven.

Availability to God demonstrates that you have a proper view of God in your life.

Witness for God

When you see God for who He really is, you will also be a witness for God. The people who really saw God in Scripture gave their lives to declaring His message. Like the apostle Paul, who saw Jesus Christ on the Damascus Road and then gave his life trying to bring other people to saving faith in Jesus Christ, if we have an accurate view of God, we will share Jesus Christ with those who do not know Him personally.

Christianity has come a long way. The tragedy is that much of it has been the wrong way. Listen to Christians talk today. They talk about a new book they have read. They talk about a new truth they have learned in Scripture. They talk about a great ministry in their church. They talk about what they learned in their last Bible study. They talk about a concert or seminar they attended recently. They talk about their Christian friends. They talk about a new Christian song. They talk about the most recent Christian CD they purchased. They talk about a new computer software program they discovered that will help them learn the Bible. They talk about a new Christian Internet site they came upon while surfing the net.

This is amazing! Rarely do you hear Christians talk about the most recent experience they had in sharing the gospel with a person who needed Jesus. Rarely do you hear Christians talk about a lost person with whom they sense the Spirit of God wants them to share the gospel. Rarely do you hear in prayer circles Christians requesting prayer for a lost person they are trying to win to faith in Jesus Christ.

Why is this happening? This is so foreign to what burned within the hearts of those who saw God. This is foreign to those who saw the resurrected Jesus Christ. I submit to you it is happening because of an improper view of God. We need to rescue God and His character from distortion and maintain a proper view of Him that will lead us to share His message of love and forgiveness to people without Jesus.

When your view of God is accurate, you will be available to God and a witness for Him. Few things fan the fire within more than seeing people won to faith in Jesus Christ.

Just recently, I equipped four hundred of our people to share their faith. They met with me for twelve Tuesday nights. After each equipping session, we sent them out into the community to share Jesus. When we had our celebration time, sharing what God did in the visits, the place became electric. On one evening alone, we saw twenty people come to faith in Jesus. Everyone was elated, and the presence of God was overwhelming in that place.

Every time I lead someone to faith in Christ, my heart is thrilled. Few things provide me with such fire and power! It ignites my life as few things can.

BECOME A GREAT COMMISSION CHRISTIAN

The last words of Jesus to His disciples are known as the Great Commission, recorded in Matthew 28:18–20: "All authority has been given to Me in heaven and on earth. Go therefore and make disciples of all the nations, baptizing them in the name of the Father and the Son and the Holy Spirit, teaching them to observe all that I commanded you; and lo, I am with you always, even to the end of the age."

It is clear that Jesus wants us to be involved in sharing His message to all persons around the world who do not know Jesus Christ as Lord and Savior. He wants us to be involved in making disciples by going, baptizing, and teaching.

Be a Great Commission Christian. A Great Commission Christian is a witness for God. As you become available to God, you will become mobile to witness for God. Give your life to being a Great Commission Christian.

Do not play the "gift card" by saying, "Evangelism is not my spiritual gift." Do not play the "theological card" by saying, "If God wants them saved, He will save them, even without me." Do not play the "making-disciples card" by saying, "My spiritual gift is making disciples, not winning souls." Do not play the "deeper card" by saying, "Evangelism is shallow. I prefer getting deep with God." Each one of these expressions and beliefs occurs because of an improper and weak view of God.

A proper view of God will result in your sharing the good news of Jesus Christ with people who do not know Jesus Christ as their personal Savior and Lord. This spiritual discipline needs to be deeply entrenched into our hearts, burning like a deep ember in a fire.

> A proper view of God will result in your sharing the good news of Jesus Christ with people who do not know Jesus Christ as their personal Savior and Lord.

We could not give our lives to anything greater. Sharing the good news of Jesus Christ will fan the fire within and ignite our lives with spiritual power.

CHAPTER 7

WORSHIP THAT CHANGES THE RULES

It was one of the most phenomenal days in my life. I have never seen the Spirit of God so evident among God's people. Expectancy filled the air. As we worshiped, the presence of God was almost visible. The liberty of the Holy Spirit was so evident among us. The fear of the Lord reigned upon the place. It was a day I will never forget—June 4, 1995. The experience and events of that day transformed our church forever.

Under God's mighty hand and direction upon my life, I yielded to a very clear call from God. God had called me to fast and pray for revival in our nation, in our church, and in my life. This was not the first time I had fasted and prayed over these burdens. Yet this time was different. The fast was not a one-day or three-day fast, but God had called me to fast and pray for forty days. Words cannot describe what happened in my life during those forty days. I wrote about it in depth in my book, *The Power of Prayer and Fasting*. In short, those were forty days that changed my life.[1]

Toward the conclusion of those forty days, when I knew God had profoundly spoken to me, I began to seek the Lord about whether I should share this experience with the congregation I pastored. I knew without question that the Spirit of the Lord was giving me clear direction and clearance to do so. I felt the message was clear. "Gain some of your strength back. Inform the people of your deep desire to share some of your life with them." Therefore, the target day became June 4, 1995.

I tried to use meaningful discernment in those days leading up to that Sunday. I felt that I needed to take a few small groups of people through a glance at what God had done in my life. In addition, I wanted to bring them alongside of me in prayer because I felt with all my heart that God was going to move in a profound manner. I wanted them to be ready to receive it. However, my overall goal was to ask them to partner with me in prayer for that targeted day.

The day came. My heart was ready to burst like the prophet Jeremiah's when he declared that the message of God was like fire in his bones. When we were in the beginning of worship, the Holy Spirit ushered Himself into the room and sat down among the people. Unless you have been a part of something like that, you would tend to think my words to be mystical and extreme. Think what you want. God was with us. He began to envelope the entire congregation as we worshiped. Just before I spoke, our choir sang with great passion a song entitled, "Lord, Have Mercy." That day, the mercy drops of heaven were showering upon us. The glory of God was there.

As I began to share the calling of God upon my life during the forty days I spent with God and the testimony of what God did in me, the audience listened intently. God had prepared the people, and I knew He was up to something very special. Since I had walked into places I had never been with God in my personal worship during those forty days, I knew that God was about to let our congregation cross over into places we had never been as a church. It was one of those days when we wanted to go farther than we had ever gone with the Lord. Nothing was going to hold us back.

While I was preaching, the glory of God came down. I felt as if I were watching God deliver His message before our people. I told them what God had shown me about America and about our church. However, I told them more about what God had shown me about my life. Much of it was not pretty. In the middle of the message, the power of God was overwhelmingly evident. I told the people I felt I needed to speak as long as God wanted me to that day and not to be held captive by another Sunday school that was to start at 11:00 A.M. following our 9:30 A.M. worship service. The people affirmed with applause and shouts of "Amen." God was there in a way they had never seen, and they did not want to miss Him. On that day, the rules had changed in worship.

Even before the public invitation was given, hundreds of people flooded the aisles. There was extreme brokenness over sins. There was outward weeping and wailing. There was silence. It was profound and holy. God was there. The public invitation began, and it seemed as if fresh and continual waves of the Holy Spirit kept rolling into the room. I did not want to mess up anything God was doing, so I felt as though I was walking on holy ground.

It was after noon, and God's people had been in holy awe for two and one-half hours. No one wanted to leave. The glory came in a new way as we began to move into true and meaningful celebration. This was extraordinary. It was unlike anything I had ever been a part of in my life. Was it planned? Absolutely not! No person or experience could have done or brought upon God's people what happened on that day. The rules had changed in worship.

I challenged the people to come back that night and pursue with me what God might want to do with us. I told them we would wait upon God and be with Him as long as He desired. Seventy percent of the people returned on Sunday evening. I told you, the rules changed in worship!

> Seventy percent of the people returned on Sunday evening. I told you, the rules changed in worship!

Great expectancy was in the air, and a buzz about what God had done among us that morning filled the hallways. Our evening service seemed to pick up right where we had left off that morning. Celebration was in the heart of God's people. It was not long until God directed us toward quiet and holy moments with Him.

I felt impressed by the holy God of heaven that our local body of believers needed to be cleansed. I sensed that I needed to give time for people to confess their sins before the Lord. When our church had been smaller, we had at times opened things for testimonies, but we had not done it in years because of the size of our membership and the risk that someone might destroy what we had desired God to do. But on this night, I put aside all those negative risks, knowing that God wanted to do something. I had no idea how to handle it but determined to be like a quarterback at the line of scrimmage and audible along the way.

You have got to see it with me for a moment. There was no laughing. There was no side talking. There was no judgment. From small children to senior adults, the holy God of heaven had called us to attention.

After giving a few guidelines, I opened up the microphones to the people. A woman came and confessed a very unique problem. After her two-minute confession, I felt that God told me to have her kneel at the altar. Then I sensed God lead me to see if there were any other people who were dealing with this same sin. I asked those people if they would like to come forward, acknowledging that sin and kneeling beside the woman who had given the public confession. Many came. Men and women alike. Then I asked people to come and pray over them in the grief of their sin. As a congregation, we went right on to the next sin being confessed. The body ministered to the body. It was extraordinary!

On that evening we saw weeping as we had never seen in public worship. We heard sins confessed that probably shocked the Pharisees and Sadducees of my church. The freedom to share was not abused. God was there. The only time I sensed that someone was about to abuse it, I gently rebuked the person and asked people to come and pray for that person.

It was a God happening! On that night, the rules had changed in worship. After sensing that God was closing the evening after deep confession and prayer, God led us into an extraordinary segment of outward praise with song. It seemed it all had just begun. Yet it was past 10:00 P.M., and we had been there at least four hours. No one wanted to leave. But God had given us specific instructions to bring matters to a close.

What a day! I will never forget June 4, 1995. On that day, our church got a new pastor without even changing pastors. On that day, I got a new church without even changing churches. God had moved as none of us had ever seen or experienced. People who were there on that day will never forget the impact of that day upon their lives and our church. No one could deny it—God met with us. On that day, the Holy Spirit fanned the fire in our lives through worship.

The news soon traveled all over America about what God had done. Churches across the nation have shown the videotapes of that morning's service. Some have shown it to their entire church in worship services, praying that God would give their people an appetite to see God move.

The Holy Spirit is very creative. The Word of God gives Him plenty of room to work within the confines of Scripture. He never works the same from week to week. Yet, when we sensed the wave of His Spirit blowing our way, we rode the wave. We still do.

Since that day, when the rules changed in worship in our church, it has been an extraordinary ride. We have seen deep revival, great spiritual warfare, and unprecedented evangelism. Today we stand stronger as a church than we have ever stood, experiencing greater growth and depth than we have ever had in our 130-year history. Our people today give their lives and resources to take the gospel to the ends of the earth. We believe this commitment to be a Great Commission Church full of Great Commission Christians can be traced back to June 4, 1995—the day that God came and changed the rules in worship.

DEFINING WORSHIP

When Jesus talked with the woman at the well in John 4, He challenged her about authentic worship. He told her that true worship would only happen when she worshiped God in spirit and truth. The word *worship* in the passage is the Greek word *proskuneo*. The word means "to do reverence to, to fall down and worship, or to prostrate oneself." Little twenty-first-century worship, privately and corporately, is following this clear word from Jesus on worship.

When I was in those forty days of deeply seeking God in 1995, I asked God to enlighten me about this subject of worship. He led me to experience it personally and privately before the definition came to me one day. Of course, what God had given me, if it was truly from Him, would also be within the boundaries of Holy Scripture. If human experience is not filtered through the Word of God, it is not God who is giving the experience. Remember, our ultimate authority is Scripture, not our experience or our tradition.

The definition of *worship* God gave me is that *worship is an encounter with Christ that results in lifestyle change.* Would you read that definition again? Consider it. Meditate upon it before you continue reading this chapter.

There is no worship without a personal encounter with Christ. He is the center of our worship. He must be encountered. This is why the Bible has such a great emphasis on worship. The Bible reveals the Living Word, Jesus Christ. Christ is always encountered in real worship.

When you encounter Christ, you will worship. When you encounter Christ, you will never be the same. Your life will change. Some areas of your life will change because you have been in the presence of God. If you have not experienced a lifestyle change, you have not worshiped.

There are two marks of real worship that are very important for you to remember: an encounter with Christ and a lifestyle change. These are pivotal in worship, or it has not really existed.

You can sit still in worship, raise your hands to the heavens, clap your hands, run through the aisles, or hang from the chandeliers, but if you do not leave with a specific area of your life being changed by God,

> You can sit still in worship, raise your hands to the heavens, clap your hands, run through the aisles, or hang from the chandeliers, but if you do not leave with a specific area of your life being changed by God, you have not worshiped.

you have not worshiped. You can sing hymns, praise choruses, and worship tunes or have a band, a praise team, or an orchestra, but if God has not changed a part of your life, you have not truly worshiped.

Let me synthesize all of these thoughts for you. When you truly encounter the living Lord Jesus Christ in worship through the proclamation and reading of God's Holy Word, some part of your life will be altered. The Holy Spirit will transform you into greater Christlikeness. When you truly encounter Him, there will be moments when you fall down and worship Him. Moments when you prostrate yourself before a holy and righteous God. Moments to say nothing or do nothing but experience His awesome presence, giving reverence to Him in every way. This kind of worship will fan the fire that God has placed into your life.

WE ARE MAKING THE WRONG THINGS THE ISSUES

Many churches in the American culture are going through major transition in their worship ministries. Some of the transition is healthy, but some of the transition is very unhealthy. In our desire to get the attention of unsaved people, we may have miscalculated the importance of some things, placing some good things on the altar of building a great crowd. Some of this may have come at the expense of destroying a church. The trade-off is questionable.

In many circles, there are still major dialogue and sharp disagreement over whether you should sing hymns or choruses in worship. What is working in another church in the region or across the country seems to be what many see as the solution to spiritual deadness. As well, dialogue is continual about the place of outward expressions in public worship, such as raising hands, clapping hands, kneeling, or coming to the altar.

I am convinced we are making the wrong things the issues. The issue is not whether you sing hymns or choruses. The issue is not whether you use drama or dance. The issue is not whether you raise or clap your hands. These are not the main issues. Stop letting the evil one, Satan, sidetrack you into this game that no one wins.

The issue in personal and corporate worship is much greater. There is such a vacuum in understanding a true theological perspective of worship that we do not even understand that the rules have changed in worship. Our goal is to meet Christ. How we get there is not the issue! When we meet Him, God will give us a new song. He will begin to move us toward our ultimate goal: Christlikeness.

Let me capsulize what I am saying in a succinct and clear statement for you: *Our destination in worship is not where we worship or the way we worship, but our destination in worship is the God we worship.*

Stop making your destination hymns and choruses, clapping or raising hands, drama or dance, or outward expressions of worship. Those matters will take care of themselves in God's time for you personally and for your church corporately, once you truly encounter God in worship. God is your ultimate destination in worship. If you miss Him, nothing else really matters at all.

A WORD FROM THE LORD

A stirring passage in Scripture that is very relevant to both private and public worship is 2 Corinthians 3:12–18:

> Having therefore such a hope, we use great boldness in our speech, and are not like Moses, who used to put a veil over his face that the sons of Israel would not look intently at the end of what was fading away. But their minds were hardened; for until this very day at the reading of the covenant the same veil remains unlifted, because it is removed in Christ. But to this day whenever Moses is read, a veil lies over their heart; but whenever a man turns to the Lord, the veil is taken away. Now the Lord is the Spirit, and where the Spirit of the Lord is, there is liberty. But we all, with unveiled face, beholding as in a mirror the glory of the Lord, are being

transformed into the same image from glory to glory, just as from the Lord, the Spirit.

The gospel of God found in God's Word clearly teaches that salvation is received through Christ alone. In Him and Him alone is our salvation. Discussions of something different from this were recorded in Acts 15. The discussions were that salvation was Christ, plus keeping the Law. This was a fierce debate among some, and it impacted other areas of church life, especially worship. The council of Acts 15 did confirm that it is Christ and Christ alone for salvation.

If Christ alone is the way for salvation, then Christ alone is the way for worship. The Law had its place and still has its place, but the day of it dictating worship has come to a close, as demonstrated in 2 Corinthians 3:12–18.

Let me lead you to evaluate, in a biblical and practical way, when the rules change in worship in your life. When you realize they have changed and adapt to the changes in your life, it will set your life on fire.

WHEN DO THE RULES CHANGE IN WORSHIP?

In Moses' adventure to Mount Sinai, he encountered God in a life-changing way. God had impacted his life greatly, and He continues to influence us through the Ten Commandments.

When Moses came down from the mountain of God, his face was radiant. The glory of God was upon him. The farther Moses moved from this mountaintop experience, the more the glory of God faded from his face. Therefore, Moses put a veil over his face so the people would not notice that the glory was fading.

To this very day, the Jews' minds are hardened to the true gospel of Jesus Christ. They are so bound to the Law of God that they are missing the fulfillment of the Law, Jesus Christ. They read the Law continually and operate their lives by it. Just as Moses had a veil that covered his face, the Jews have a veil that covers their hearts. Just as

Moses' veil covered his face and kept the people from seeing the glory fade, the Jews have a veil over their hearts that keeps them from the truth of the gospel of Jesus Christ. This is why their worship is bound to the past and to the Law, rather than to Jesus Christ, the entire Word of God, and the Holy Spirit.

Many people who profess to be Christians in the American church are in the same place. They are bound to their past traditions and have a hard time seeing the whole truth. They are more committed to their religious tradition than they are to the truth of God.

> Many people who profess to be Christians . . . are more committed to their religious tradition than they are to the truth of God.

The answer for every person is worshiping God in the right way. The rules have changed in worship. Let's look at when the rules change in the way we worship.

Turn to the Lord

The rules change in your worship when the veil is taken away. When a person turns to the Lord, the veil is taken away, as 2 Corinthians 3:12–18 tells us. The word *turn* is referring to a time in your life when you repent of your sin, come to the Lord in faith, and experience a changed life by the grace of God. When you make that strategic and pivotal decision in your life, the veil (whatever it is that hides you from the truth about worship) is taken away.

This is what you need to see. When you came to Christ, the rules changed in worship. When you came to Christ, you were set free from the bondage of the Law and the traditions of men. You are now in Christ! It is not Jesus plus anything. It is only Jesus. He is your standard. He defines the boundaries by His Word. He is the subject of your worship. Man-made traditions are to be tossed out the window.

Let me illustrate the contrast that has now occurred in your life since you came to the Lord. The rules have changed. Notice how they have changed on the following table:

Old Way of Worship	New Way of Worship
Tradition	Christ
Law	Spirit
Condemnation	Acceptance
Bondage	Liberty
Death	Life
Result: Preservation	Result: Creation

The old way of worship was ruled by tradition, while your new way of worship is ruled by Christ. The old way of worship was determined by the Law (or your human or religious traditions), while your new way of worship is directed by the Spirit of God. The old way of worship resulted in your condemnation, while the new way of worship results in your acceptance into the Beloved. While the old way of worship places you in bondage, your new way of worship grants you spiritual freedom. The result of the old way of worship is death, while the result of your new way of worship is life. Do not let this one pass you by: While the old way of worship is always trying to be preserved for whatever reason, your new way of worship is creative as the Holy Spirit leads and dictates within the boundaries of God's Word.

When you turn to the Lord, your worship is not centered on yourself or on some tradition, but upon Jesus Christ. He is the center of your worship. It is not centered on you and your needs. It is not centered on a form of tradition that your church follows. It is centered on Jesus Christ. When Jesus is the center and you encounter Him, your needs are secondary, as well as your religious tradition.

The performance-based American society has negatively influenced the church. When this performance-based mentality is permitted to enter the worship of churches, the self-centeredness is increased. Pride is very deceitful. It leads us to outward display for human recognition. There is something I have told our people since 1995 that I want you to consider. *When pride walks on the platform, God walks off.* God shares His glory with no one. Jesus is to be the center of our worship.

Twenty-first-century worship in the American church needs to take a very sober and evaluative look at worship. Churches have now designed specific worship services to target certain desires or needs of people. If meeting the needs of people is the goal, then worship will not be experienced. True worship is Christ-centered, not self-centered. Whatever happened to our belief in the power of God? Does this mean that churches should not consider the people in a worship service? Not necessarily. We should just make sure that we are not giving people another "quick burn," rather than Jesus. Jesus in full will solve all matters. He is enough! When He is lifted up, people of all ages, backgrounds, races, nationalities, cultures, and generations are brought unto Him.

When We Taste the Presence of the Holy Spirit

The rules also change in worship when we taste the presence of the Holy Spirit. Jesus said in John 4:24 that "God is spirit." Second Corinthians 3:17 says, "Where the Spirit of the Lord is, there is liberty." This means you have freedom in your life. You are no longer dominated by the Law or traditions of men, but by the Spirit of God. The Spirit of God is the presence of the Lord or the glory of the Lord.

Once you taste of the Holy Spirit, the rules change in worship. When the powerful wind of God's Spirit blows upon you, everything changes. This is what happened to me during my forty-day fast and what happened to our church on June 4, 1995. The wind of God's Spirit blew, and the rules of worship changed.

What I have discovered is that the degree to which you experience the Holy Spirit and His control in your life will be the degree to which you experience various degrees of worship. The degree to which you experience the Holy Spirit, you experience free-

> The degree to which you experience the Holy Spirit, you experience freedom in worship.

dom in worship. By the way, when this freedom happens, it is always within the boundaries of God's Word. In addition, you permit others to worship in the way they choose. You do not have to be judgmental, telling everyone else that they are doing it wrong. If you have this attitude, you are not encountering Jesus in worship, but you are worshiping yourself.

This is why different churches worship in different degrees. Each has experienced various degrees of the Spirit of God upon their church. This is why it is very immature to try to place within your church what someone else has done in theirs. You have to let the Holy Spirit customize His own experience for your church. He will determine how you are to worship. Then your church will be more in the flow of the transitions He creates. I am not sure that singing gets us into the anointing of God's Spirit. I am sure that once we are under His anointing in worship, He determines the songs we sing.

Pursue God. Taste the presence of the Holy Spirit of God. Let Him determine the songs in your life and your church.

When We Are Transformed by the Glory of God

Second Corinthians 3:18 verifies that the glory of God is the presence of God. Everyone who comes to the Lord has the veil lifted. The veil represents whatever is keeping you from coming to the Lord. When this veil is lifted at salvation, it remains lifted. This is when the rules change in worship. Once you invite Christ into your life, you will no longer go back to any past format of worship. Everything changes. Your traditions and personal preferences fall along the wayside. Jesus is your focus.

When the veil is removed, you gaze in the mirror of the Word of God. As you gaze in the mirror and live according to the Word of God, the Holy Spirit transforms you. As you look into God's Word, you see God's Son. When this occurs, the Holy Spirit transforms you. This is right in context with Jesus' teaching on worship in John 4:23: "But an hour is coming, and now is, when the true worshipers shall worship the Father in spirit and truth; for such people the Father seeks to be His worshipers." The Spirit is the Holy Spirit and the Truth is the Word of God. True worship does not exist without either one. Remember, both the Word and the Holy Spirit always point you to Jesus Christ.

When you experience this powerful worship experience in your private life or in a local church worship service, you are transformed into the image of Jesus Christ. The transformation does not take place outwardly until it happens inwardly. Worship sets your life on fire. As life is taking place within you, God begins to work on the outside. You not only live from the inside out, you worship from the inside out.

As you experience the glory of God in worship, you become more like Jesus. The presence of God has changing power upon your personality. Your ultimate goal is Christlikeness. That only happens when you worship. The spiritual discipline of worship ignites you inwardly and then ignites every phase of your life. It fans the fire of the Holy Spirit that is in you.

Each person is on a different level of spiritual growth. As you encounter Christ, your lifestyle changes. This happens from glory to glory, which means you experience various levels of sanctification or Christian growth. This only occurs as you worship.

Are you being transformed by the glory of God in your life? This happens when you worship the Lord Jesus and the Holy Spirit changes you in accordance to what God's Word is doing within you. The more the Word is working in you, the more the Holy Spirit conforms you into the image of Jesus.

You may wonder about the Holy Spirit's place in personal and corporate worship. As you study the Scripture, the involvement of the Holy Spirit is essential for worship to occur. He is the One who works within you. He is the One who illumines God's Word for you. He is the One who points you to Jesus Christ.

The involvement of the Holy Spirit is essential for liberty to exist in worship. The involvement of the Holy Spirit is essential for your transformation into Christlikeness as you worship. The Holy Spirit is the One who ignites you to experience spiritual power. The Holy Spirit is the One who changes the rules in worship. Let God's Spirit transform you through worship.

QUICK TIPS FOR PERSONAL AND CORPORATE WORSHIP

I want to conclude this chapter by giving you a few quick tips for your personal worship of God, as well as the worship you experience with God's people.

Beware of Offering Strange Fire in Your Worship

According to Numbers 3:4, Nadab and Abihu, the sons of Aaron the high priest, died when they offered "strange fire" before the Lord. The judgment of God came upon them when they attempted to offer something to God that was not appropriate. It was something that may have had the appearance of acceptability, but was very unacceptable to God. The description of fire as "strange" indicates it was an unusual and abnormal offering. It was their simple and subtle attempt to change the rules in worship of God. They were punished with death.

The lesson in private and corporate worship is for you to beware of offering strange fire to God. God is clear on what He wants from you. Overall, He wants your life completely. He is clear that He is not into "quick burns," but He is into the spiritual disciplines that become deep burning embers in your life.

Cease substituting what God really wants from you with something cheap and plastic. Make sure you are not offering strange fire to God in your personal and corporate worship experiences. To keep anyone other than Jesus central in worship is offering strange fire to God in worship.

> To keep anyone other than Jesus central in worship is offering strange fire to God in worship.

Jesus Is Central in Your Worship

Your focus in worship is not a singer or a preacher or a plan. Your focus in worship is Jesus Christ. Attention to human personality is needless. The attention is on Jesus Christ. Work hard at not bringing attention to yourself in any way. Point people to Jesus. He is the only One we worship.

The Word of God Is Foundational in Your Worship

If the Word of God is not involved in your worship, it is not true worship. The Word of God is your foundation. It is your support. It is the pillar of truth. All other things that are called worship or pretend to be worship are only valid as to the foundation being the Word of God. If your worship is not driven by the power of God's Word, it will only be another "quick burn" in your spiritual life.

The Holy Spirit Is Life in Your Worship

If the Holy Spirit is not involved in your worship, there is no worship. He is the life of worship. Deadness, neutrality, mediocrity, and indifference happen in your personal and corporate worship because of a lack of dynamic involvement of the Holy Spirit. On-fire Christians are controlled by the Holy Spirit, and on-fire churches are controlled by the Holy Spirit.

Worship sets your life on fire. When you encounter Jesus Christ in worship, your lifestyle changes. The change is a transforming change that comes from within you. The spiritual discipline of worship practiced daily in your personal life and expressed weekly through your local church results in your life being ignited on fire. Worship fans the fire of God within you. When you are changed into Christlikeness through worship, the rules change automatically.

Get your eyes off the form of your worship and onto the substance of worship, Jesus Christ. Encounter Him, and you will experience lifestyle change. This is true worship that changes the rules.

CHAPTER 8

EXCHANGING YOUR MIND

Few things are as painful as church conflict. There are moments when it seems that church would be okay if it were not for the people. I have been there as a member, as a pastor, and as a mentor.

The apostle Paul knew how it felt to go through church conflict. Through the work of God in his heart and in the followers of Jesus at Philippi, he was hurting over reports coming to him about the church experiencing conflict. As always, there was a threat to the unity of the church that came from false teachers. But his major concern had to do with a conflict that arose between two women. He said in Philippians 4:2: "I urge Euodia and I urge Syntyche to live in harmony in the Lord."

Euodia and Syntyche were rivals. These two women were well known and influential in their church. They were also trouble.

Euodia and Syntyche were leading factions of people against one another. Their personal rivalry had turned into church conflict. The potential for major church conflict must have existed or the apostle Paul would not have mentioned their problem and names in his letter to the church. What was the problem?

No one can pinpoint a specific issue that was the point of major contention, but there are a number of possibilities. Each of them may have wanted to be the president of the women's ministry. Maybe the decision was about to be made, and their personal ambition caused a major stir. Perhaps Euodia and Syntyche wanted to teach the women's class in the church. Maybe each was trying to flaunt her teaching talents before the people, trying to win the support of the pastor of the church. Perhaps they wanted to be on the praise team during worship. Maybe Euodia was chosen and Syntyche was not. Therefore Syntyche was out telling people that she could sing better than Euodia and that the only reason Euodia was chosen was because she was a friend of the pastor's wife. Their extreme jealousy of one another may have triggered this battle.

Whatever the problem was on the outside, God pinpointed the real problem happening within them. Since the call was ringing clearly in Paul's letter to all of the Christians in Philippi, you can conclude that pride was present, selfishness was vogue, conceit was obvious, vainglory was the goal, and promotion was evident.

In Paul's clear rebuke and gentle call to the church, he shared that the Lord was their partner through all conflict in life, even church conflict. He encouraged them as he called them with great passion to be like-minded. He wanted Euodia and Syntyche, as well as the rest of the church, to be one-souled. He wanted their hearts knit together so they would have the same goals and desires. He wanted them to love Jesus and His church more than themselves and their personal agendas. I can just imagine what Euodia's and Syntyche's responses were when Paul confronted them.

Paul's ultimate goal in writing to the church about this problem was to get everyone in the church to evaluate Jesus Christ. He is the one whom Paul held up as the model in life and attitude. He wanted them to exchange their minds for the mind of Christ.

THE EXCHANGED-MIND CURRENCY

One of the real challenges of international travel is understanding the financial currency of the country where you are located. The problem is increased if language is a barrier. The real key to dealing financially in other countries is to understand the exchange rate, or the worth of the American dollar in that country. For example, the American dollar is worth more in Canada than it is in Germany. The worth of the American dollar in that country determines the exchange rate, whether it is to your advantage or disadvantage.

Let me tell you about an exchange that is indescribable. The Bible says in Philippians 2:5, "Have this attitude in yourselves which was also in Christ Jesus." The ultimate challenge from Paul to these two ladies and to the church was to exchange their minds for the mind of Christ. The exchange rate that God offers you in this verse is to your great advantage. It is too good for you to pass up.

The call from God to you is the same as it was to Euodia, Syntyche, and the church in Philippi. The call is to exchange your mind for the mind of Jesus Christ. You are to have the same mind, attitude, and thoughts as Jesus Christ. The great news is that God is willing to place His mind, attitude, and thoughts in your life. What a great exchange!

If you want to add another deep ember to the fire within in your life, you have no other choice than to exchange your mind. The spiritual discipline of exchanging your mind for the mind of Christ will fan the fire within. Nothing has a greater potential to dampen the fire more than holding on to your own mind, attitude, and thoughts.

> Nothing has a greater potential to dampen the fire more than holding on to your own mind, attitude, and thoughts.

The Battlefield of Your Spiritual Life

You might think that the battlefield of your spiritual life takes place every day while you are out working and operating in the world. It is a major battle, but it is not the key battlefield. I want to challenge you never to forget the following statement: *You will win or lose your walk with God on the battlefield of your mind.* This is why the apostle Paul issued the challenge in Philippi to exchange our minds for the mind of Christ.

You can have a time with God daily and walk in spiritual defeat. You can attend worship weekly in your local church and walk in spiritual defeat. You can attend a Bible study during the week and walk in spiritual defeat. All of this can happen if you miscalculate where the battle will take place.

The battlefield for your spiritual life is your mind. You will win in your spiritual life if you understand where the most strategic battle is going to take place and take action to prepare for it. The secret to winning in the Christian life is exchanging your mind for the mind of Jesus Christ. Exchanging your mind for His will lead you to spiritual victory. Maintaining your mind in the Christian life will result in continual spiritual defeat.

Where is this battlefield in your mind challenged?

Education

The educational system in America is very unfriendly to your spiritual life. The academic circles wear their intellectual arrogance rather well. Their tendency to intimidate their students results in prejudice toward Christianity. Their liberal mind-set results in left-wing practices that are permitted with little or no regret. They evangelize innocent minds with their philosophical jargon and court anyone who will not resist. Some of them are referred to as "the intellectual elite," due to the wealth of knowledge they love to parade before others.

God is not the center of their teaching; man is the focus. When a Christian walks into their battlefield, he or she should be ready for major battle. The tragedy is that the children and youth of our country have little, if any, choice to anything other than receiving this kind of education.

Thank God for Christian teachers and administrators in public and private schools and universities who have a different world-view than the institutions in which they are teaching. Thank God for their sacrifice in making an investment in the next generation. If you are a Christian teacher or administrator, I encourage you not to be blindsided by the system. Stand unashamedly for your faith. Demonstrate courage in every decision. The Lord is with you.

Therefore, the challenge for us as parents is to train our children to have the mind of Christ. As we walk onto the educational battleground, we must ensure that our children have exchanged the mind of Christ on their own personal battlefield, their minds. The challenge for parents is also to be involved in the school that the child is attending. Do not put on blinders, but be as wise as serpents and as harmless as doves. Those of you who are gifted with leadership and courage, run for positions of influence such as the school board in your community. Do it for the children of your region, as well as for your own children. They are at risk! However, it is imperative that you do this with the mind of Jesus Christ.

Family

The family is also a battleground for your mind. Is your family friendly to your living with the mind of Christ? The only hope for your family is to live with the mind of Christ.

One of the major reasons tragedy is striking in families across America is the mind-set of the family. Many families, even professing Christian families, are as vacant as most educational institutions are of the centrality of Jesus Christ. If Christ is not the central person in your home, you are opening yourself up to major disruption by Satan. If Jesus is central, your family will pray together. Do you ever pray with your family? If not, do not gripe about being unable to pray in public schools.

Be careful what you permit in your home. Ungodly magazines, improper videos, questionable television programs, and potentially dangerous Internet sites will choke the fire of God from your life and family. Why? Because they promote a mind-set that is contrary to Jesus Christ. Would Jesus read those magazines, watch those movies, view those television shows, or browse those Internet sites? Absolutely not! Determine to have in your mind what is in His mind.

Train your children to have a daily time with God to put on the mind of Jesus Christ. Encourage and lead them in Scripture memorization, which will be dependable weaponry on any battlefield. Pray for your children to put on the armor of God daily. Pray with them every day before they leave for school. Train them to exchange their minds for the mind of Jesus Christ.

Media

The media venues in America are brainwashing people with a mind-set that is contrary to the mind of Jesus Christ. They have become a big exclamation mark to the liberal intellectual elites in America.

Through television, the media determines the way most Americans think about politics, education, health care, family, and even Jesus Christ. Television is powerful! It can rapidly lead you astray. It will promote to you everything other than the mind of Jesus Christ.

Through billboards, the minds of the American population are challenged. The open sensuality you see on billboards while driving on the roads of America is difficult to believe. Keep focused while you drive, or you may lose the battle for your mind.

Through radio talk shows, you are saturated with the opinions of the hosts and those who call in. Isn't it amazing what you hear? You almost never hear anything to affirm your faith or family values. Instead, you hear what others think about all issues. Be a breeze of refreshment by calling in with Christ's perspective.

Friends

The kind of friends you keep will determine many things in your life. Make sure you run from so-called friends who do not exhibit the mind of Christ. Do all you can to run with intensity toward friends who have the mind of Christ. I will deal with the issue of friendships more in depth in the next chapter.

Way of Life

Be careful of the places you go in your life. Are they friendly to the mind of Christ? Would Jesus go there for the same reason you would go there? If you do not exchange your mind for

> Be careful of the places you go in your life. Are they friendly to the mind of Christ? Would Jesus go there for the same reason you would go there?

the mind of Christ daily, then you will be swallowed up by the world. Yes, you have to live *in* the world, but you do not have to be *of* the world. This is why this great exchange is needed.

The educational system and its institutions, the family, the media, your friends, and the way of life you pursue are all battlegrounds in your life. However, you will win or lose your walk with God on the battlefield of your mind. This is your major battlefield, and you will do well never to forget it.

EXCHANGING YOUR MIND FOR THE MIND OF JESUS CHRIST

Every day is a struggle for me. I go through the same challenges that each of you goes through in life. One of the biggest struggles I have is winning the battle in my mind. Like you, I live in a world that bombards me with a mind-set opposite to that of Jesus Christ. I receive the same attacks that you do in your life, attacks that challenge my desire to be sexually pure and holy before God. By God's grace, I have made it. His angels have stood for me when I did not even know it.

A few years ago, I began to understand the critical nature of having my mind under control from early in the morning to late in the evening. I knew that if I let my guard down just one time at an inappropriate moment, I could lose my spiritual life and ministry. I knew I needed to establish a new spiritual discipline in which I would exchange my mind for the mind of Jesus Christ. Yet I did not know where to start.

One day in my study, it all came to me. When the apostle Paul addressed the church conflict in the Philippi church, he gave them what I needed most: He pointed them to Jesus. He challenged them to develop the same kind of mind that Jesus demonstrated through everything in His life.

That day, I realized that I have to live with an exchanged mind. My mind will lead me to sin and death. The mind of Jesus will lead me to peace and life. I began to look intently into the life of Jesus Christ as recorded in Philippians 2:1–11. If the Christians in Philippi needed to exchange their minds for the mind of Jesus, so did I. If Christ is our model, then I need to look at Him closely and emulate the mind of Jesus Christ.

I want to highlight three key features in the life of Christ that have to become a part of our lives. This is what you will exchange your mind for every day.

THE UNSELFISH CHRIST

As Paul dealt with the problem of Euodia and Syntyche, he told them to be as unselfish as Jesus. He commanded, "Do nothing from selfishness or empty conceit" (Phil. 2:3). The Christians in Philippi and the Christians in our world are to do nothing from selfishness.

Euodia and Syntyche were seeking something for their own glory. They were promoting their own interests with great intensity. This selfishness is referring to factions and divisions that were the fruit of selfishness. Attempting to bring honor, praise, attention, or recognition to yourself is selfishness.

Selfishness occurs because of pride. It is when you choose "my life," "my desires," or make a statement like, "It is my way or the highway!" These are all indicators of selfishness.

Notice how Paul pointed the Christians in Philippi to Jesus Christ. In Philippians 2:6, he wrote, "Although [Jesus] existed in the form of God, [He] did not regard equality with God as a thing to be grasped." If anyone had the right to be selfish, it was Christ. Jesus was in the form of God. He was God in His deepest essence, nature, and being. Jesus was and is God. Even though Jesus was equal with God, He did not try to hold on to or grasp being God. He did not claim His rights, privileges, abilities, and equality with God; instead, He released them all for a season to be the Savior of the world.

What a great model of unselfishness Jesus is for you and me! If we are going to exchange our minds for the mind of Jesus Christ, we had better begin with discarding personal selfishness and embrace the unselfishness of Jesus Christ. Our goal should be unselfishness, denying the ambition to promote ourselves in any way. Easier said than done.

This call to unselfishness will affect your life in every way. Everything begins with what you really believe about yourself. It is important that you believe you are not God. You are just one person. You are not a perfect person. When you choose to promote yourself, it is because you believe deeply that you are worth talking about. Let others do it. You stay quiet.

> When you choose to promote yourself, it is because you believe deeply that you are worth talking about. Let others do it. You stay quiet.

When you are unselfish, you will not say statements like, "I am better than them," or "I am going to take this into my own hands," or "I will do whatever has to get done," or "I do not care what they think about it!" These statements represent a very selfish attitude. Self is never to be on your agenda, and selfishness is never to be your motive.

When you are selfish, your family experiences conflict. The source of conflict in your family is pride and selfishness. Taking up for yourself or defending your position are ways that selfishness tends to create conflict in your family. Sometimes it is more profitable to say nothing than to say something that is rooted in selfish desires. Family living is improved when you die to your opinion. Life can go on, especially in the family, without your always giving your opinion.

When selfishness is tolerated in your life, you may create disruption in the church. If you hang on to your selfishness, you may stir up gossip, backbiting, conflict, rivalry, schisms, and divisions in your church. All of these things are very un-Christlike. None of them should be acceptable to you. The only way to guard yourself from causing sin in the church is not to be selfish.

Be sure you are not a source of conflict in various relationships in your life, such as with friends, people in the community, and on the job. Selfishness in you can create conflict with any relationship you have.

The unselfish Christ is our model for unselfishness. The Scripture affirms this again in Romans 15:3, which says, "Even Christ did not please Himself." What a challenge. Our goal should be to please Christ, not ourselves.

The Humble Christ

Chuck Swindoll writes the following about the humble Christ:

> The Greeks said, "Be wise, know yourself."
> The Romans said, "Be strong, discipline yourself."
> Religion says, "Be good, conform yourself."
> Epicureanism says, "Be sensuous, enjoy yourself."
> Education says, "Be resourceful, expand yourself."
> Psychology says, "Be confident, assert yourself."
> Materialism says, "Be possessive, please yourself."
> Asceticism says, "Be lowly, suppress yourself."
> Humanism says, "Be capable, believe in yourself."
> Pride says, "Be superior, promote yourself."
> *Jesus Christ says, "Be unselfish, humble yourself."*[1]

I love that quote. It cuts to the heart of the matter. Christ was unselfish and humble, and we should follow His example.

Paul went on to challenge the believers in Philippi and believers today by writing, "With humility of mind regard one another as more important than yourselves; do not merely look out for your own personal interests, but also for the interests of others" (Phil. 2:3–4). The direct opposite of desiring human praise is the heart of the word *humility,* which means "to be lowly and humble." Scripture acknowledges that we are to regard others as more important than ourselves.

When you have humility of mind, the attention is not on you, but on others. Other people, other interests, other goals, and other dreams are more important than yours. This is why the success of others is more important than your own success. Do you give your life to making others successful? This is the heart of the Christian life.

Paul's description of the humble Christ continues in Philippians 2:7–8, which says, "[Jesus] emptied Himself, taking the form of a bondservant, and being made in the likeness of men. Being found in appearance as a man, He humbled Himself by becoming obedient to the point of death, even death on a cross." Jesus emptied Himself of the outward display of deity. He refused to promote His own interests, and He refused to use His divinity for personal gain. This is the picture of the humble Christ.

Just as a king would exchange his kingly robe for sackcloth in times of mourning, Jesus exchanged His deity for humanity for a time. Yet He was fully man and fully God. He may have appeared to be just a man, but He was so much more—He was God! Hanging on the cross between two thieves and dying like a criminal shows His shame and His humiliation. This was His complete and perfect sacrifice for the sins of the world, including yours.

People today are looking for a cheap cross. I heard about a missionary in South America who was visiting a shopping area, going from booth to booth. As he was browsing and examining the goods, he saw a sign above one booth that said: "Cheap Crosses."

There is a trend among Christians today that is frightening. Although these people have good intentions, they attempt to make their messages appealing to the world by never mentioning the need for sacrifice. This is in complete contradiction to Jesus and His Word.

There is no such thing as a cheap cross. That statement is an oxymoron. The cross of Jesus was not cheap; it cost Him His life. This is why a humble person does not run *from* sacrifice, but *to* sacrifice. Christianity is about sacrifice. It is about being humble. This is the mind of Christ for which we exchanged our minds.

When you are humble, you are driven to others, knowing they are more important than you and your agenda. When you are humble, you are involved in service, knowing Jesus displayed a servant's heart. When you are humble, you are inspired to sacrifice as Jesus did. Whatever the cost is to you personally is no longer the issue. The issue is that you want to be like Jesus.

Are you willing to embrace this type of Christianity? It is the only real Christianity. Anything other than this is a mere imitation of the real thing. When you exchange your mind for the mind of Christ, you are putting on an unselfish and humble mind. This will set your life on fire.

THE EXALTED CHRIST

God does not share His glory with anyone, including you and me. Jesus is the only One whom God has exalted. This is recorded in Philippians 2:9–11, which says, "For this reason also, God highly exalted Him, and bestowed on Him the name which is above every name, so that at the name of Jesus every knee will bow, of those who are in heaven and on earth and under the earth, and that every tongue will confess that Jesus Christ is Lord, to the glory of God the Father." Because Christ was unselfish and humble, God chose to exalt Him.

God exalted Jesus above and beyond anyone and anything else. Even though His earthly career was characterized by humiliation and denial, God has exalted Him highly. Jesus is the Savior of the world. What a name! He is the Lord of all as He is the sovereign ruler over everything. Therefore at the name of the Lord Jesus Christ, all of heaven, all of earth, and all of hell one day will worship. No one is to be wor-

> God exalted Jesus above and beyond anyone and anything else. Even though His earthly career was characterized by humiliation and denial, God has exalted Him highly.

shiped other than Jesus Christ. For all of eternity, the universe will worship Him.

First Peter 5:6 says, "Therefore humble yourselves under the mighty hand of God, that He may exalt you at the proper time." This verse pictures the life of Jesus Christ. It portrays the mind that should be exchanged daily.

If you want to go up in your life, you have to begin by going down. This is what Jesus did. He humbled Himself and then He was exalted. This spiritual truth is still true for you. Exchange your mind to be unselfish and humble. When this happens with the purest motive, God will lift you up at the proper time.

Do you have the mind of Christ today? Are you thinking and living unselfishly? Are you thinking and living humbly before God and others? Are you thinking and living with the kind of faith that it is up to God alone to exalt you in every facet of your life?

It is a supernatural event for you to exchange your mind for the mind of Christ. It happens daily and even throughout the day. The only way that will ever happen is through God's power, because you cannot think your way into unselfishness and humility.

Therefore, when you pray, exchange your mind for the mind of Christ. Daily ask God to make this exchange for you. When you read the Word of God, put on the mind of Christ while you are reading it. Just say to God, "I want to be like You. I want to think the way You think. I want to feel what You feel. I want to see what You see." When you think, think upon things that are godly and holy.

The kind of things we should think about and dwell upon are emphasized in Paul's closing words to the church in Philippi: "Finally, brethren, whatever is true, whatever is honorable, whatever is right, whatever is pure, whatever is lovely, whatever is of good repute, if there is any excellence and if anything worthy of praise, dwell on these things" (Phil. 4:8). Every one of these things is a characteristic of the Lord Jesus Christ. Each feature is to be thought about continually by followers of Jesus Christ.

When Do You Start?

The place of beginning is very important for everything in life. It is important to know the date of your birth because it was the beginning of your life. It is important to know your anniversary because it was the beginning of your marriage. It is important for you to know the date or the season of your spiritual conversion because it was the beginning point of your Christian life. Beginnings are important in almost everything.

Even though it is important for you to know your birthday, anniversary, and your spiritual conversion, I am not sure anything is more important than what I am about to tell you. The starting place of exchanging the mind of Christ is the moment you have a thought. Train yourself to reach out and grab it. Second Corinthians 10:5 says, "We are taking every thought captive to the obedience of Christ."

You can do this by capturing your thoughts, one by one, as you have them. Instantly place them under captivity so that you can obey and honor Christ. You do not win the battle for your spiritual life after your thought has become an action. You win the battle for your spiritual life the moment you have a thought of any kind. Take it captive and put it under Jesus Christ!

This will take great spiritual discipline. It will take a supernatural act as God's Holy Spirit is living through you ushering every thought to be under Jesus' leadership. This is the way you exchange your mind for the mind of Christ. You gain everything and have everything to lose if you do not do it. Remember: You will win or lose your walk with God on the battlefield of your mind.

When you elevate the spiritual discipline of the exchanged mind, the Holy Spirit will fan your fire. I guarantee that this spiritual discipline will ignite your life.

CHAPTER 9

FINDING YOUR OAK

As I get older, I have a greater desire to reproduce my life in others, especially ministers of the gospel. I have a real passion to place within others the spiritual disciplines that God has placed into my life through the years. Few things bring me more fulfillment than when I am able to see this accomplished.

For a number of years, I have watched the struggles of some of the younger men who serve in our staff. Our church has a large staff team that encompasses every ministry and mission in our church. From this multiple staff, there are twenty-one men I have classified into this younger category. A few are not married, some are newlyweds, and others have been married a few years and have the joy of preschoolers and young children.

For quite a while now, I have been meeting with these twenty-one men once a month. In this two-hour meeting, we visit with one another while eating lunch, discussing everything from football to the family. After lunch is completed, we move into a share time of what God is doing within them and their ministries. The final seventy-five minutes of the meeting, I teach them about various things in life and ministry. We conclude our meeting with a question-and-answer period.

Every time we meet, we experience a growing camaraderie in friendships and ministry. The fellowship is becoming stronger as we pray for one another. I receive reports from these men and their spouses of how various areas of their ministries and marriages are improving. This meeting fans my fire. Even though the preparation is extensive, detailed, and time-consuming, I walk away from that monthly meeting very fulfilled because I have made an investment in others.

My goal is to be their friend, not just their pastor and leader. My goal is to challenge them spiritually to go to a higher plane. My goal is to sharpen their ministry skills so God can use them greatly. My goal is to encourage them through whatever problems they are facing personally, in their family, or in the ministry. My goal is to provide them with a greater accountability so they can seize the higher ground in life and ministry.

I want to be a burning ember to their spiritual lives so they will burn longer and hotter for God. I want to fan their fires so they can burn brightly to others. I want to ignite their lives by modeling before them the powerful spiritual disciplines of the Christian life. I want to be like a piece of oak wood in their fire.

WOOD FOR THE FIRE

In the first chapter, we discussed the importance of building a fire. If the fire is built properly, the fire will burn longer. The kind of wood you place into the fire will determine how long and how hot the fire burns.

> The kind of wood you place into the fire will determine how long and how hot the fire burns.

Once the twigs have helped the base of the fire start effectively, it is critical that the wood placed on top will become deep embers that will burn long and hot. Even if you have little experience in building a fire, you know this to be true and essential.

If you use cedar wood in the fire, you will hear it crackle! It will sound really great. Initially, it will also look astounding because it will burn brightly. The only problem is that the leaping flames will not last long. It is nothing more than a quick burn just as paper is to a fire.

If you use cotton wood in the fire, it will add virtually nothing. It is so full of water that it will not season. Therefore, it will not burn.

If you use green wood in the fire, it just does not burn. You can add quick burns to it continually, but it is not seasoned enough to burn.

But if you use oak in the fire, it will burn as long and as hot as any wood. In time, it will become embers to your fire. It will glisten with red and orange flames that make a beautiful fire.

WOOD AND YOUR FRIENDS

Does this wood remind you of any of your friends? I want you to think deeply with me about how this wood represents the kind of friends you have.

Some of your friends are like cedar wood to your spiritual life. They are nothing more than quick burns. They charged into your relationship with great intensity, but they fizzled out of your life just as quickly. Here today, gone tomorrow. These types of friendships are brief because their motive is receiving, rather than giving.

Some of your friends are like cotton wood. Just as cotton wood looks promising but cannot burn, these friends make promises they cannot keep. They are full of Christian sayings and appearances, but they add nothing to your friendship. More tragically, they add nothing to your spiritual fire.

Some of your friends are like green wood. They are immature and unable to burn. They have not been seasoned with life and the things of God. You just cannot count on them. Like your cotton wood friends, they add nothing to your spiritual life. You had hoped they would help you burn brightly for God, but you had to become the fire in their lives. The problem is that it does not matter how long you try to help them; they do not want to grow.

Perhaps you have a few friends who are like oak wood to your spiritual life. They put some things into you that make you burn longer and hotter for the Lord. They are the fan to your spiritual fire! They ignite you spiritually. If you have a friend who is like an oak to your spiritual life, you are very fortunate.

PAUL AND HIS FRIENDS

As a traveling preacher, the apostle Paul had many friends. He not only won many people to Christ, but he also met some wonderful Christians throughout his journeys. I want to highlight some friends Paul had through his ministry as well as share about what kind of friend Paul was to others.

Demas Was Like Cedar

Everyone needs the kind of friends who will walk with us through all kinds of circumstances, the type of friends who will be deep embers within our lives and who can fan the fire within us. Unfortunately, every friend does not do that for us, and we do not serve as embers to every friend we have in life.

Paul had a close associate named Demas, with whom he had walked through some meaningful times. One day, Demas had all of costly Christianity he wanted. In 2 Timothy 4:10, Paul gives the sobering news of his friend's departure from the faith: "Demas, having loved this present world, has deserted me and gone to Thessalonica." Demas could not remove the attraction of the world from his life. He loved the present world more than he loved the things of God.

Finally, Demas deserted the apostle Paul and went to Thessalonica. Paul was left in a difficult position of need when Demas abandoned him. Once a friend and associate, Demas became a deserter to the man of God. Tragically, Demas never counted the cost of his discipleship.

Demas was like cedar wood to the fire of God within Paul. He came into Paul's life with great zeal and left just as quickly. Just as cedar burns brightly for a moment and then is gone, Demas gave the appearance of being a loyal friend and then deserted Paul. The cost of being Paul's friend was great. Paul was a passionate and courageous leader who was not pursuing popularity in this world. He wanted to be a great man of God who pleased Christ. This is why Demas became like cedar wood to the fire within Paul's life—here today, gone tomorrow.

Even though the Scripture does not give details concerning the feelings of Paul when Demas deserted him, I am confident that he was deeply hurt. I know

> Some of my darkest days in life and ministry have been when the Demases of my life have abandoned me—sometimes without notice.

what it feels like to have friends or even companions on your staff team come quickly into your life and leave just as quickly. They come with many loud crackles and flames, but they are soon off and running somewhere else. Why? The cost is just too great. The price is more than they wanted to pay. Just like Demas, they walk! Some of my darkest days in life and ministry have been when the Demases of my life have abandoned me—sometimes without notice.

I want to challenge you not to be a Demas to someone else. Do not be like cedar wood is to a fire. Do not be just a quick burn to someone else because the hurt can be great. Rise above being a Demas to a friend and rise above the Demases in your life.

John Mark Was Like Green Wood but Came Back Around

Prior to Paul's first missionary journey, he and Barnabas decided to take a young man along with them known as John Mark. This young man accompanied them to Antioch and Cyprus, but he left them at Perga. His abrupt departure did not play well with Paul. Perhaps John Mark got homesick or simply tired of working in his young age. He was young and green, not a man of season and maturity.

When Barnabas approached Paul about taking John Mark with them on the second missionary journey, Paul refused. The Scripture records this in Acts 15:37–39: "Barnabas wanted to take John, called Mark, along with them also. But Paul kept insisting that they should not take him along who had deserted them in Pamphylia and had not gone with them to the work. And there occurred such a sharp disagreement that they separated from one another, and Barnabas took Mark with him and sailed away to Cyprus." John Mark must have demonstrated such immaturity that Paul would not give in to Barnabas's desire. Perhaps John Mark's actions at the time were not the only determining factor in Paul and Barnabas determining to separate. Paul was an apostle, and his authority should have had more bearing on Barnabas being under his leadership, but it did not. Therefore, disagreement occurred between these two men of God.

Paul was a focused and hardworking servant of Christ. John Mark left when Paul was counting on him. Paul may have determined that it was not in the best interest of John Mark to go with them because of the tremendous demands and even threats on their lives. I assume this, coupled with John Mark's immaturity, led to the sharp disagreement between Barnabas and Paul.

John Mark was like a piece of green wood to Paul. He could not burn brightly because he was not seasoned enough to do so. Just as green wood is immature and needs time to reach a seasoned status, John Mark needed time to grow. For obvious and private reasons, Paul thought it was not best for the mission or for John Mark for him to accompany them.

The great news is that, in God's timing, John Mark did mature. Later in John Mark's life and Paul's ministry, Paul affirmed him as a companion in ministry. In fact, in Colossians 4:10, Paul says, "Aristarchus, my fellow prisoner, sends you his greetings; and also Barnabas's cousin Mark (about whom you received instructions; if he comes to you, welcome him)."

While Paul was in Rome, John Mark was with him. Earlier it had not been God's timing for John Mark. Now it was God's timing. At a later time, when Paul was in his second imprisonment at Rome, he requested for John Mark to come and be with him. Second Timothy 4:11 records Paul's request: "Pick up Mark and bring him with you, for he is useful to me for service." Yes, John Mark did gain the confidence and favor of Paul in completeness. In case you were wondering, Barnabas and Paul became friends and colleagues again. We learn this from 1 Corinthians 9:6, in which Paul refers to Barnabas as his partner in ministry. Reconciliation and unity had come to their relationship.

You may have friends who are like green wood to your life. They are immature, and deep friendship with them is just not possible. Perhaps you are on two different levels in your spiritual lives. Even though it may not be time for the friendship now, stay open to God about what He may want to do in the future.

I learned a great lesson many years ago as a friend and pastor. A wise man once encouraged me never to let anyone get outside of my circle of love. He said always to be willing to let them back into the circle even after they had departed from me. I have made that a practice in my life for many years. Even as people have left the circle of love, I have seen them return. My attitude of love and acceptance made the difference in their return. I am so glad I received that wise counsel many years ago.

This is exactly what Paul preached and lived throughout his life. Had he not operated out of that conviction in his life, John Mark and Barnabas would not have returned to working with him. What a lesson!

By the way, John Mark became a real champion for God. Even though he had been like green wood in Paul's life for a certain season, Paul had been like a piece of oak in his life. The result was that John Mark was the author of the Gospel According to Mark in the New Testament. What an amazing story!

Luke Was Like Oak

You may have never imagined or known that Luke was like a piece of oak wood to the fire within Paul's heart. He was one of the few, perhaps the only one over a long time, who was the oak in Paul's life. In 2 Timothy 4:11, Paul says, "Only Luke is with me." Luke was a close companion and friend to Paul.

Luke was a physician. His training made him think like a scholar and be detailed in his writing. Luke was the author of the Gospel According to Luke. He was also the author of the New Testament Book of Acts. In the Book of Acts, you will see occasional references to "we" or "us," in which Luke is referring to himself and Paul. He was with Paul from Acts 14 and beyond. You will not find Luke's name written down in the Book of Acts, only his references to "we" or "us," indicating himself and Paul.

Luke provided for readers of the New Testament a documented, detailed account of the founding of Christianity to Paul's imprisonment. As you read the entire New Testament, you will discover the excellent and detailed writing of Luke. He must have been a very gifted researcher to provide such detail. These writings verify the depth of his walk with God and his commitment to the evangelization of the world.

So what was Luke to Paul? He was a very close friend who experienced much of life with Paul. He traveled with Paul throughout most of Paul's ministry. As much as Paul was beaten up for the gospel, he must have been grateful to have had his own physician accompanying him.

Luke must have been a deep ember to Paul's life. Strong men like Paul have few men who can be a continual source of strength to them. Luke's writings demonstrate that he had the depth in the Lord to be like a burning piece of oak wood on the fire of Paul's heart. Luke was with Paul through all of the difficult times and picked Paul up when he needed to be picked up. He must have been this kind of close friend and companion to Paul, or they would not have made it long with one another, since the tribulation was so great. Luke was a deep ember to Paul, putting something into his life that would make Paul burn longer and hotter for God.

Without question, Paul was a great man. Many say he was the greatest Christian in the New Testament. Perhaps Paul was such a great man because of a man like Luke who was a piece of oak on his fire.

Paul Was Like Oak

Paul was a deep ember in the lives of many great New Testament Christians. He would put something back into the lives of people that would make them burn longer and hotter for God.

Paul was like oak in the life of Silas, who accompanied Paul in much of his traveling ministry. Probably the best-known account of

Silas is his jail stay with Paul as recorded in Acts 16. They were singing at midnight when God performed a miracle: He opened the prison for them. Paul and Silas led the jailer and his family to Jesus Christ. Silas was a great man of God. Paul was like oak in his life.

Paul was like oak in the life of Luke. Their depth with God was mutual. Their friendship was great. They were oaks to one another through much of their lives and ministries. It is obvious that Paul had incredible influence on Luke's life.

Paul was like oak in the life of John Mark. Paul's rejection of John Mark's immaturity may have been the very thing that God used in John Mark's life greatly. Something had changed because Paul received him back and John Mark had grown in his depth in order to write his gospel. Paul motivated John Mark spiritually to go deeper and farther with God. He was like a burning ember in John Mark's life that made him burn longer and hotter for God.

Paul was like oak in Timothy's life. Paul loved Timothy and began investing in his life while Timothy was in his late teens or early twenties. The love and admiration were mutual, but without question he mentored Timothy in the things of God. The two Books of Timothy that are in the New Testament record Paul's deep feelings for this younger minister of the gospel. Paul made Timothy burn longer and hotter for God and was an oak in his life.

Paul was oak in the lives of many churches. Many of the New Testament books are letters that Paul wrote to various churches. His influence did not just reach into the lives of a few men of God, but to countless numbers of people. He founded churches. He mentored churches. He loved these churches. He was their encouragement—a burning ember to their fire.

If Paul served as an oak for many people and churches, just think what an oak could do for your life. Someone who would motivate you to go farther with Christ than you have ever been.

> If Paul served as an oak for many people and churches, just think what an oak could do for your life.

WHAT AN OAK CAN DO FOR YOUR LIFE

I want to inform you what an oak can do for your life. The list is beyond human comprehension, but let me highlight just four things an oak can do for your life.

Be a Friend Through Everything You Face in Life

A person who is an oak will go with you through everything you face in life. A friend who is like an oak to your spiritual fire will not desert you in the midst of trouble. This friend will not desert you through the various transitions that all friendships encounter and will be with you through everything you face in your life.

My wife, Jeana, has a friend named Debby. When Jeana went through her cancer experience some years ago, Debby walked through it with her. I called Debby the night that I knew Jeana needed some major reassurance about the future. One of the reasons that Debby is an oak to Jeana and Jeana is an oak to Debby is because time and the experiences of life have built that strong relationship. Even though schedules with children and family may separate them for segments of time, immediate fellowship occurs when they rejoin one another for a brief luncheon. You see, Debby has walked through some deep water with Jeana. Their friendship is strong because they are like oak to one another.

A person who is an oak in your life will be with you through the trials of your life. They will pull up their bootstraps and go with you through whatever God takes you through in your life.

Spiritual Challenge

Remember, a piece of oak in a good fire eventually becomes a deep ember that brings incredible longevity and heat to the fire. Even when the oak has become an ember and begins to burn down for a period of time, it puts something back into the fire that will make it burn longer and hotter.

That is exactly what someone will do for you as an oak in your life. They will make you burn longer and hotter for God. They will challenge you to go to a new level spiritually. They will motivate you to go places you have never been. Their life will encourage you to go to the higher ground they live on, regardless of the personal cost to you.

They become the "iron" of Proverbs 27:17, which says, "Iron sharpens iron, so one man sharpens another." Each person needs another person to sharpen him or her. Who is sharpening you? Whom can you dialogue with about deep spiritual things? Who can say you are wrong about an issue? It is helpful to have someone in your life who can sharpen you.

Just as Luke sharpened and challenged Paul, you need someone who will motivate you to go to another level with God. Someone who will challenge you to go to spiritual heights you have never imagined yourself going. Someone who will place within your life a greater passion for God and His kingdom.

Encouragement

You need someone in your life who will instill courage in you. Someone who will lift you up and help you face everything in your life when you would prefer to quit. Someone who will encourage you when you are even doing well. Someone who will encourage you to go to that next level with God even when you have reservations about going.

Who is your source of encouragement? Does anyone do this for your life?

Barnabas was known as "the son of encouragement." He had a gift of lifting people up and motivating them to have more courage, regardless of what they were facing. I do think there is a valid lesson to learn about encouragement from Paul and Barnabas's relationship. Even though Barnabas was a great encouragement to Paul, you cannot live on encouragement alone. A relationship has to have depths of trust and loyalty, even beyond encouragement.

This should call you to understand the value of balance in a friendship. A true oak will be all of these things to you and more.

Accountability

The word *accountability* has become a buzzword in Christian circles. There are some who think that accounta- bility to someone else is a guar-

> Deceit can be used in any relation- ship, even those that have the per- ception of great spiritual depth.

antee that failure will not occur. This is idealistic thinking, because even some of the great Christian leaders who have fallen had all kinds of levels of accountability, including their own little group where the hard questions were asked. Deceit can be used in any rela- tionship, even those that have the perception of great spiritual depth.

In spite of this, you need accountability in your life. An oak in your life will provide you the needed spiritual accountability. They will provide you moral accountability. They will provide you practical accountability.

They will hold you accountable to move to the next level once you have stated you want to go there. They will not let you get by with mediocrity and bland neutrality. They will hold your feet to the fire.

For some time I have met with a trainer two days a week. He has motivated me to work out five to six days per week. He has been good for me. He holds me accountable in the details of exercise. Form is so important to strength training. If I do not do it right, he makes me do it until it is done right. Do I pay someone to make me accountable in having the proper exercise, fitness, and nutritional program? Yes! You might say, "Well, I can do that on my own." I hope one day to achieve your strong level of accomplishments in exercise, fitness, and nutrition. However, what I have observed is that without accountability, these areas will be sacrificed and many times ignored completely.

Just as someone motivates me with an exercise program, we need people in our lives who will motivate us spiritually. We need someone who will hold us accountable in every way.

Is it possible to find someone who will be a friend to you through everything you face in life? Someone who will challenge you to go to a new level spiritually? Someone who will encourage you? Someone who will hold you accountable? I believe it is, and I want to show you how to find one.

HOW TO FIND YOUR OAK

Now that I have shown you biblically and practically what someone who is an oak in your life can do for you, I want to show you how to find one in your life.

Pray for an Oak

It is clear to you at this time the value of having a person who is an oak to your spiritual life. There are scriptures to verify the blessings and challenges of having an oak in your life. You can stand on them before God in prayer.

Stop looking for an oak as if you are searching for a job. Take God's approach. Pray for an oak to come into your life. Pray for it to be very clear to you about who it should be. Pray for God to bring this person into your path. Pray for the person to be open to God about it. Above all, pray for God's timing because His timing is essential in all matters, even in finding an oak.

Initiate Friendships

You will not find your oak by prayer alone. You have to spend time building relationships with others. You have to initiate friendships with people. You have to ask them into your home or out for a meal. Stop waiting on someone else to initiate friendship with you, and take the initiative in establishing and nurturing friendships.

You will discover the oak in your life through one of these relationships. He or she will emerge from these friends in God's timing. If you look at these friendships and determine an oak is not present for you, you have to initiate more friendships. Does this mean you ignore the ones you have already established and nurtured? No, but it means the circle has to be widened. In God's timing, He will bring an oak into your life. The chances are that this oak will likely emerge from a friendship in your life.

Look in the Right Places

If you are going to discover a true spiritual oak for your life, you have to go where the oaks are. I believe I know where oaks hang out.

People who are oaks hang out in God's house. They are in the church walking with God and growing in their faith. They are Great Commission Christians who are involved in sharing the gospel somewhere in this world. They are in active service in their church, making a difference with their lives. They are not Sunday morning Christians, but strong servants who are paying the price in serving the Lord's church far beyond Sunday morning. They are givers who actively support the ministry of the church with great zeal and commitment. Oaks hang out in churches that are pastored by oaks. Hang out in the church and you will discover oaks who are like deep embers in a fire.

Another place oaks hang out is with other oaks. Someone has made them great for God and that is the person they want to be with in their lives. Only an oak can keep an oak going strong. This is why they become as resilient embers in a burning fire. These resilient embers compose friendship and churchmanship. The two go together and are inseparable. Therefore, where one oak is, another is close by. Go and see if they will let you hang out with them for a while.

Approach Them

An oak always responds to someone who has a deep burning zeal in his heart to follow God. Now if it is someone who is just leaning on them to be a better father or worker, forget it. Oaks do not compartmentalize life. They see life as a whole, where Jesus is the center of life. They believe that as your spiritual life goes, so goes the rest of your life. They are not motivated by buzzwords like *accountability*. They are motivated to invest their lives in people who have a great burning zeal to grow for God and already show evidence of some spiritual growth. Oaks do not have the time or passion to put up with immaturity.

So if you are already growing with passion and fire in your walk with Christ, wanting to be a difference-maker, then approach an oak. How do you approach an oak?

> So if you are already growing with passion and fire in your walk with Christ, wanting to be a difference-maker, then approach an oak.

Ask him for a specific time when you can share with him privately. Get in an environment with him where you can have his focus. Keep the time to a reasonable length, keeping the oak's schedule in mind, not yours. Let him extend the time, not you. Share with him your desire to find a spiritual oak for your life. Be honest about where you have been, where you are, and where you want to go spiritually. Share with him that you are aware you cannot go there on your own. Inform him that you have watched his life and have been impressed with what you have seen. Ask him to consider in prayer becoming an oak to you. Tell him you are not looking for an answer today, but you want him to pray about it. Ask him if he needs to ask you any questions. Agree together on a reasonable time to determine if it is God's will for both of you. If by chance he tells you no initially, just ask him to go home and pray about it. Obviously, you should never approach someone to do this for you and with you until you have prayed deeply and effectively about it, sensing God's direction to go to him.

Leave it all in God's hands. He has a person and a time for this in your life. Be patient and let Him do His work in you.

A FINAL WORD

My friend Jamey Ragle serves as a full-time evangelist and is one of the most humorous and effective communicators I have ever heard. He is like medicine to the soul. Jamey once said to my church: "Show me your friends and I will show you your future."[1]

Those are powerful and profound words. Look at them again. Let them sink deep within you. This is why you should do your best to hang out with oaks in your life. Your spiritual life will be determined greatly by the type of people you hang out with in your life.

Spend your time being with people who are like deep embers in a fire who make you burn longer and hotter for God. They will fan the fire within your life. Set your life on fire by finding an oak for your life.

When this spiritual discipline concerning friendships, especially finding an oak, exists in your life, you will go farther with Jesus than you have ever gone before. The great news is that you will have someone who is walking with you to that higher ground.

CHAPTER 10

FAITH IN THE FIRE

On January 15, 1990, I began to walk in a dimension of faith I had never been before. On this day my wife, Jeana, was diagnosed with cancer. I had demonstrated faith in the fires of personal struggles and the challenges of church life. However, I had never been challenged to let my faith live in the midst of life and death.

This is not a story about Jeana's cancer experiences, but a story about faith in the fire. Within days of that initial diagnosis, I sensed God drawing me to Him through this experience to teach me about faith in the fire.

I sensed God's great calling to fast and pray one day a week for Jeana's healing. It was on one of those days, soon after diagnosis, that the Lord spoke to me through His Word. The words came from Isaiah 43:1–3:

> Do not fear, for I have redeemed you; I have called you by name; you are Mine! When you pass through the waters, I will be with you; And through the rivers, they will not overflow you. When you walk through the fire, you will not be scorched. Nor will the flame burn you. For I am the LORD your God, The Holy One of Israel, your Savior.

I knew this was God's word for our situation. I knew this was the promise I was to claim in these uncertain days.

Upon that Scripture, I began to stand. I stood in prayer. I stood in prayer and fasting. I stood with family. I stood with friends. I stood with our church. I stood with other intercessors. God's word to me was that He was going to heal her. I was operating with faith in the fire.

The object of my faith was God. I knew He controlled life, death, and the struggles in life. The basis of my faith was the Word of God. God never lies. What He says, He means. I believed this was God's personal promise to me for Jeana's survival in the fire.

Therefore, I held that word through doctors and hospitals. I held that word through surgery. I held that word through reports. I held that word through radiation treatments. I held that word through chemotherapy treatments. I held that word when it was all completed. I held that word through the procedures medical experts felt were successful. Everywhere I went through those months, those Scriptures were on a card that I carried in my pocket.

I learned that you cannot have convictional and believing faith without God's Word. I was trusting God regardless of what happened to Jeana, but I knew God was going to heal her—and He has! It has been more than ten years from the date of the initial diagnosis, and she is still free from all cancer. To God be the glory!

My faith did not heal Jeana; God healed Jeana. What God gave me from Isaiah 43:1–3 were the necessary words to get us through the challenge of having faith in the fire. In that greater dimension of faith, I have grown in my faith. My faith was developed in the fire.

Whatever you may be going through in your life, be assured that God will give you faith in the fire. Regardless of how intense the fire of your trial may be, pursue God to give you the word and the power to get you through the trial of your fire. Just as I was willing to accept the circumstances and the results of whatever God wanted to do with my wife, I was willing to stand with faith, leaving it all in the hands of God.

This chapter will instruct you about faith, but it will also motivate you to have faith in the fire. This kind of faith pleases God. It is the kind of faith that fans the fire of God in your heart.

What Is Faith in the Fire?

I want to provide you with a working definition for faith in the fire. I believe it is the kind of faith that pleases God. What is faith in the fire? *Faith in the fire is positive obedience to the Word of God, regardless of the circumstances and results.*

Let me explain to you. The Word of God is essential to faith in the fire. If you do not have a word from God about what you are going through in your life, then you cannot demonstrate positive obedience. The positive obedience to the Word of God can happen because of your great belief in God and what He says in the Bible, His Word. This will occur when you saturate your life with God's Word.

Faith in the fire involves a great commitment. The commitment is that you are going to obey God in a positive manner, regardless of how hot the circumstances get around you. You are not going to shrink away from your faith, but you will exert great faith in the fire. The commitment also involves your living with the results. Whatever happens, you will stand on the Word of God. Even if the prayer is not answered and what you sensed God was going to do does not occur, you are going to operate with great faith in the fire.

The Word of God serves as the hope you have through the fire. It is God's assurance to you that He is moving. He is moving before the fire, in the fire, and even after the fire.

How much do you need the Word of God in your life? It is a constant need. Remember this: *You are either going through a storm, you are in a storm, or you are about to go into a storm in your life.* Life is one constant storm. Thank God for the periodic breaks, but the storms of life serve as our fiery trials. God wants to provide for you the kind of faith that gets you through the storms of life.

> Life is one constant storm. Thank God for the periodic breaks, but the storms of life serve as our fiery trials.

This is the kind of faith that exhibits positive obedience to the Word of God, regardless of the circumstances or results. Is this kind of faith really possible? Yes, and I want to show you how.

A Story of Faith in the Fire

The Bible is full of stories about people who walked through the fires of life. One of my favorites is recorded in the Book of Daniel. Let me introduce you to Shadrach, Meshach, and Abed-nego, three Jews exiled in a foreign land.

King Nebuchadnezzar of Babylon made an image of gold and set this image up as being a god. He gave instructions that when the instruments played, everyone was to bow down and worship the golden image. He also instructed the people that if anyone failed to fall down in worship of the image, they would be cast into a furnace of blazing fire.

The king received reports that three Jews refused to bow down and worship the image. The king brought the men before him. He was going to give them another chance, so he explained in detail what they must do when the instruments played again. He told them that no god would be able to rescue them from the furnace of fire.

Even before the instruments played again, Shadrach, Meshach, and Abed-nego told King Nebuchadnezzar that they still refused to bow down to his false god. They knew that their God, the true God, was able to deliver them from the fire and out of the hand of the king's judgment.

Their actions and words so angered the king that he instructed his servants to increase the fire's heat by seven times. The men were tied up with their clothes on and thrown into the fire. Although the heat of the fire alone would kill the men, they were tied up to ensure they could not escape the flames.

While watching the fire burn, the king asked his servants if only the three men were put into the fire. His servants confirmed that only Shadrach, Meshach, and Abed-nego had been thrown into the fire. The king looked again, and notice his response: "Look! I see four men loosed and walking about in the midst of the fire without harm, and the appearance of the fourth is like a son of the gods!" (Dan. 3:25).

Nebuchadnezzar could not believe his eyes. Instead of three men burning in the flames, he saw *four* men walking in the fire who were not harmed at all. From his view, it appeared that the fourth man had an appearance of a god.

Immediately the king came close to the entrance of the fire and called for Shadrach, Meshach, and Abed-nego to come out of the fire. They stated that they were servants of the Most High God. The servants and leaders, including Nebuchadnezzar, could not believe that the fire had no effect on the men. Their hair was not singed, their clothing was not damaged, and the smell of fire was not on them.

The king began to bless the God of Shadrach, Meshach, and Abed-nego for sending deliverance through an angel. He also announced that anyone who dared to speak an offensive word to these men would be killed. The king made sure the three godly men prospered in Babylon. In time, the king began to believe in God.

This is a story about faith in the fire—literal fire! Faith in the fire is positive obedience to the Word of God, regardless of the circumstances and results. Shadrach, Meshach, and Abed-nego knew the Scriptures. They knew there is only one true God, and He is a jealous God. They knew they could not bow or bend to a false god. They knew their lives were at stake. They knew they could die if they obeyed God, rather than the king. Regardless of the circumstances of pressure and knowing their lives were at stake, they stood on God's Word and demonstrated their faith in the one true God, not the golden image. This is faith in the fire!

These three men understood the cost before they entered the fire. They were fully aware of the possible results, yet they did not bend their knees and bow before a false god. Therefore, they were willing to count the cost.

Shadrach, Meshach, and Abed-nego are perfect illustrations of faith in the fire. They demonstrated positive obedience to the Word of God, regardless of the circumstances and results. They stood in the face of worldly authority to declare the power of their God.

It is very important to notice that they did not ask for a change in their residence. They did not declare that God would deliver them. They acknowledged that if the Lord pleased, He would be able to deliver them from the fire and from the hand of the king. These men had great spiritual maturity. Spiritual maturity is not asking God for a change in your circumstances, but for the spiritual power to be with you through your circumstances.

It is also important to know that God came to Shadrach, Meshach, and Abed-nego in the midst of the fire. He may not always come for deliverance, but this time He did. God was in the fire. God may not always come in the fires of your life to deliver you, but He will come. He will come to be with you.

This is faith in the fire—the kind of faith that sets your life on fire. The kind of faith that pleases God.

FAITH THAT PLEASES GOD

Faith in the fire as defined earlier and illustrated through Shadrach, Meshach, and Abed-nego pleases God. It is the kind of faith that delights the heart of God. This kind of faith is described in Hebrews 11:6: "And without faith it is impossible to please Him, for he who comes to God must believe that He is and that He is a rewarder of those who seek Him."

Convictional Faith

The faith that pleases God firmly believes that you cannot please God without faith. You realize that doubting does not please God. You realize that pouting does not please God. You even realize that shouting does not please God. God is pleased only when you know that faith is the only way to please Him.

This kind of faith is affirmed by the Word of God. Hebrews 11:1 says, "Now faith is the assurance of things hoped for, the conviction of things not seen." Faith is like a sixth sense in your life. It is having a conviction, or firm persuasion, because God has spoken in His Word to you. This stands beneath

> Faith is like a sixth sense in your life. It is having a conviction, or firm persuasion, because God has spoken in His Word to you.

you to support you through the fire and stands as conviction before God and others.

Much of your faith may be shallow. But faith built on God and what He says in the Bible is convictional faith. You stand in conviction that the only way you can please God is to walk by faith in whatever you go through in your life.

Believing Faith

The kind of faith that pleases God must believe that God is. It is the kind of faith that believes that God is who He says He is. He is Creator. He is Lord. He is Sovereign. He is powerful. He knows everything. He can do anything. He is present everywhere. He is God!

Believing faith is the kind of faith that believes God is everything He says He is. Do you believe that today? Regardless of the fire you are facing in your life, are you demonstrating that God is who He says He is? When you do, you will rest in His lordship, sovereignty, and power.

This is not all. Believing faith also believes that God can do whatever He says He can do. Anything God says He can do in Scripture, He can do. There is not one exception.

Does your life show that you believe God can do whatever He says He can do? For you it may be very difficult right now, but believe God! He can do anything. Let Him do in you and through you what He wants to do.

Pursuing Faith

The kind of faith that pleases God is faith that comes to God. You must pursue God in your faith. When you come to God, you will pursue God.

You need to come to God voluntarily. You need to pursue God with all of your heart. In the midst of seeking Him, you are exhausting all your powers to seek God. You are seeking God with everything you have, giving nothing to the world. Pursuing faith is the kind of faith that pleases God.

When you seek God earnestly, you will have a great reward. God will increase your faith. He will give to you convictional, believing, and pursuing faith.

This kind of faith is the kind of faith that pleases God. Are you pursuing God in your faith? Nothing is worthy of greater pursuit than the things of God and God Himself.

When you walk by the kind of faith that pleases God, you will be renewed, revived, and ignited for God. Pursue living by faith in the fire.

FAITH IN THE FIRES OF YOUR LIFE

Through God and His Word, you can live with faith in the fires of your life. I want to investigate some various fires through which God will increase your faith.

Fire of Transition

God will give you faith in the fire of transition. Life is full of changes. In the American culture, people are always in some kind of transition. Can God give you faith through your transitions? Yes!

You may be going through the transition of a new job. Your family has just moved to a new city. Initially, it does not seem like home. Everything is strange. Your husband is already busy in his new job. You are still trying to dig out of the boxes in the garage. Your children are attending a new school and tackling the challenge of making new friends. You are trying to make the best of it, but it is tough. You really feel down about it. You have prayed. You have asked friends in your previous location to pray for you. Yet, it is tough!

The fire of transition is never easy for anyone, especially a wife and mother. A new house is not yours until it is set up like yours. A mom is not happy until she knows her children are happy. Spend some extra time in the Word of God and prayer. Ask God to speak to you. He will. When He speaks in His Word, walk in it. This is called faith in the fire of transition.

Perhaps your children are just now leaving home. As a father, you would have never imagined the struggle you are having. It is just you and your wife. The house is so quiet. The evening schedule has slowed down because you are not chauffeuring children any longer or going to watch them participate in the many activities in which they were involved. You are in the fire of transition.

Things are really changing with you. This is not easy. The reality of getting older is setting in as you think about your life. As you prayed, God affirmed to you that He was in control. You know He is with you. What do you do? Walk through the fire of transition. Keep your eyes on the Lord. Renew your relationship with your wife. Talk to your children. Investigate new activities that you and your wife can do together. Most of all, live with great faith as you walk through the transition of your life.

Transitions can be multiple. Yours may be very unique right now. Live by faith. Do not choose doubt. Do not pout about where you are. Choose faith—the kind of faith that pleases God. It will get you through the fire of transition.

> Transitions can be multiple. Yours may be very unique right now. Live by faith. Do not choose doubt. Do not pout about where you are.

Fire of Loss

Faith that pleases God will also see you through the fire of loss. Few things are as devastating as loss. It becomes a part of your life the older you get. The only problem with living a long time is that you cannot live without loss.

You may be experiencing a loss in your life. You are losing your health. You are just not what you used to be. You feel it and look it. Maybe you are losing your health through an illness. You see your body deteriorating. The doctors are only saying that you are a sick person. Perhaps you have had financial loss. You have really suffered since a turn in the market. Your indebtedness is too high. You are feeling the crunch and will have to approach the family about an adjustment of lifestyle. Few things create pressure more than loss of financial security. Maybe you have just buried your spouse. The loneliness is unbearable. Your heart aches as never before. Everywhere you look in your home and drive in the community, there are memories. The loss has been catastrophic for you.

Perhaps you have just lost your spouse to divorce. He or she was unfaithful to you. Your spouse's lifestyle is deplorable, but you still love him or her. The last thing you ever thought is that divorce would occur in your marriage. The loss you feel is horrible.

Whether your loss is in one of these areas or in another area of life, your only hope is faith in the fire. Identify what God is saying to you through the fire. Take your pain to God in prayer. Keep the faith. God will see you through.

Exercise faith in the fire of loss. Remember, God is who He says He is and God can do what He says He can do. You have to believe God. Hold on to what you know God is saying. You will make it.

Fire of Uncertainty

God will also give you faith in the fire of uncertainty. Fear has gripped your heart. The future is up for grabs! Just as you had the future all planned out, this bump comes along. You cannot ignore it because it is big. It creates uncertainty in your heart about your future.

You may be single and uncertain if God is ever going to give you a mate. You may be in a financial crunch and struggle even looking toward the future. You may be moving to a new location and are fearful. Everything is so uncertain. You may be going to work in a new job. You are scared! You feel so uncertain about it even though you felt good about it when you took the job. What do you do?

The future can be frightening for everyone. You are not alone. However, you have to live with great faith as you surge through your uncertainty. Identify what is creating the uncertainty and place it before God in prayer. Let Him speak to you about it in His Word. Live by the scriptures that God gives to you. Only God can give you faith in the fire of uncertainty. If He can give to Shadrach, Meshach, Abednego, and a host of others faith in the midst of their uncertainty, He is able to do it for you.

You may be uncertain about eternity. Heaven and hell are real, and you must be prepared. God has given you the forgiveness of all your sins. You receive this free gift by demonstrating faith in Jesus as your personal Savior and Lord. I guarantee He can give you faith in the quandary of your eternity.

Fire of Obedience

God can give you faith in the fire of obedience. Even though God may speak very clearly to you about your situation, sometimes it is very difficult to obey God. It was not easy for Abraham to place Isaac on the altar. It was not easy for Daniel to walk into the lion's den. It was not easy for Jesus to go to the cross. Obedience is costly. Only faith can take you through the fire of obedience.

You may know God has confirmed that the woman you are dating is the one He has chosen for you. Yet, the struggle is great even though you love her and are very pleased with her being God's choice. You may believe that God has spoken to you about a problem in your church. God has challenged you to take the church to the high road of reconciliation. You are not directly involved in the fight, but you love your church and the people involved in the conflict. You may know God has spoken to you clearly about taking a new job five hundred miles from your hometown. You have prayed. You have sought God. He has answered, but it is tough making that final decision.

Friend, each of these situations and others like them is the crucible of your faith. Obedience to God's Word is not always easy. Sometimes it is very tough and costly. What do you do? Obey God! You have no choice. You certainly do not want to disobey God and receive the consequences, so obey God and receive the rewards.

Put your faith in the One who is the fire and makes the fire. Once the word is given to you, press on. God has been faithful to call you. He will also see you through. Be faithful in the fire of obedience. Fulfill God's Word to you. Don't look back! Great faith will take you through great fire, even the fire of obedience.

Do Not Forget This

Do not forget that faith in the fire is positive obedience to the Word of God, regardless of the circumstances and results. This kind of faith was good enough for Abraham, Noah, Enoch, Abel, Jacob, Gideon, Barak, Samson, Jephthah, David, Samuel, and the prophets. If faith got them through the various fires of life, it will get you through the fires of your life.

> Do not forget that faith in the fire is positive obedience to the Word of God, regardless of the circumstances and results.

When you live by faith in the fire, your fire will be fanned by the Giver of that faith. The spiritual discipline of faith in the fire is essential for successful Christian living. This kind of positive faith will ignite your spiritual life. As you walk in it, you will renew the fire within.

Oswald Sanders says it well when he writes, "Faith enables the believing soul to treat the future as present and the invisible as seen."[2] What a faith! What a life! What a God!

When others see this kind of faith in you, they will be attracted to the Lord. They will want your God. When someone embraces your God, it is wind beneath your wings. Fly on . . . with faith in the fire.

CHAPTER 11

NO EASY PATH

When your life is on fire, there is no easy path. The simple things become complicated. The complicated things become overwhelming.

You may have a "pie-in-the-sky-by-and-by" approach to Christian living. You may feel that things are supposed to get easier when you follow Jesus. If this is what you believe, you are probably not burning with a great fire for God in your life.

The view you or others may hold about "easy Christianity" is simply not biblical. After Pentecost, Peter burned for the Lord and faced great conflict in his life. From the moment his eyesight was restored, Paul burned brightly for the Lord and lived in continual conflict all the way to death. Stephen burned greatly with the fire of God in his heart and was stoned to death. There is no easy path when your life is on fire for God.

I can certainly testify to this. It seems that the hotter the fire burns in my life, the greater the spiritual conflict. Even after moments of being on the mountaintop, I am faced with conflict. I have never found any easy path following Jesus. The more I am on fire, the greater the spiritual conflict.

SPIRITUAL CONFLICTS

When your fire burns, you will face spiritual conflicts in your life. This reality is biblical in every way. When men and women in the Bible were burning with the fire of God, they constantly faced spiritual conflict.

Look at the life of Jesus Christ. No one in human flesh has ever burned with fire for God more than Jesus Christ. He exuded passion to be with the Father. In every way, Jesus' life burned with fire.

However, at every turn, Jesus faced conflict. The closer He got to the ultimate fulfillment of His coming—the cross—the more spiritual conflict occurred. It came from the religious audience, from Satan, and eventually from the government establishment. The spiritual conflict resulted in His death. In His life, there was no easy path.

We are to walk in the fellowship of His sufferings. Therefore, we will continually face spiritual conflicts. Since there was no easy path for Jesus, there will be no easy path for us.

The spiritual discipline you must understand is that there is no easy path when the fire burns in your life. When you grasp the full dimension of spiritual conflict, you will be ready to face it. This will result in igniting your spiritual life to go to levels you have never been with God.

IDENTIFYING THE CONFLICTS

You will face many conflicts in your spiritual life. I want to assist you by identifying the places or persons of conflict. This will prepare you and inform you for the various battles you will face.

Conflict with Satan

The first conflict I want to share with you is conflict with Satan. In the midst of pressure, it is easy to think you have many enemies in your life. Part of Satan's lie is to cast the blame on someone else. I want to reiterate something that you should never forget: *Satan is your only enemy.* You have no other enemy but him.

The Scriptures inform you of the incredible intent of Satan to come against you in your life. The Bible says in Ephesians 6:10–12:

Finally, be strong in the Lord and in the strength of His might. Put on the full armor of God, so that you will be able to stand firm against the schemes of the devil. For our struggle is not against flesh and blood, but against the rulers, against the powers, against the world forces of this darkness, against the spiritual forces of wickedness in the heavenly places.

It is very apparent in these verses that you are being called to prepare yourself for spiritual battle. You are to put on the full armor of God so you will be able to stand against the manipulative, lying schemes of Satan.

Since the Word of God is always right, notice that it identifies the heart of your struggles in life. Your struggles are not against people, circumstances, and various situations; they are against Satan. He is your only enemy. Satan and his mighty demons of hell are in an all-out war against all Christians. The war is greater toward Christians who are really burning with God's fire. His entire arsenal is pointed toward you.

The kingdom of Satan has an order. It has various ranks that are activated for various areas of service. It has a strategy. It is not a loosely connected army working through confusion, hoping to create chaos in your life; it is a very strategic army that knows its role, its enemies, and what it has to do to win.

The more my heart burns for the Lord, the more spiritual conflict I encounter with Satan. I get it every day at every turn. Nothing is easy anymore in my life. What has been orderly has become threatened with great disorder. The devil seems to be in every detail of life.

THE THREEFOLD STRATEGY OF SATAN

I am not the kind of person who looks for demons everywhere while the *Twilight Zone* theme song plays in the background. However, I am also not the kind of person to act as if Satan is no big deal. I have gotten to know Satan quite well. He has so attacked my personal life

> I have gotten to know Satan quite well. He has so attacked my personal life and ministry through the years that I have learned a great deal about him.

and ministry through the years that I have learned a great deal about him. I have observed through the years the strategies of Satan against my life and others, and I believe I have identified Satan's threefold strategy.

Satan Deceives

From the Garden of Eden until this very moment, Satan has been a deceiver. The Bible affirms this in Revelation 12:9: "And the great dragon was thrown down, the serpent of old who is called the devil and Satan, who deceives the whole world; he was thrown down to the earth, and his angels thrown down with him." Satan has deceived the whole world according to this passage. He also has a countless number of demonic agents who assist him in these deceitful ploys.

Satan is the con artist of all con artists. He disguises things incredibly well. He makes you think something exists when it really does not. He misleads very effectively. He takes one element of truth and uses it as bait by keeping the element of truth on the outside while masking the lie on the inside. He lures you with the bait of the world to attempt to captivate you.

You may be deceived right now because you are being lured toward a woman who is not your wife. Or because your husband is always so busy, you have learned to find romantic interest on the Internet in a chat room with another man. Satan may have deceived you to lead a coalition in your church to disrupt the fellowship of believers. Perhaps you are deceived to think that another job will bring some final satisfaction to your life.

Regardless of which area of your life Satan is invading, just remember, it will be deceiving. He will blind you from the real truth, making you think the sin you are chasing is the truth.

You are in a spiritual conflict with Satan, the deceiver. Wise up to his deceitful ploys. He is a scheming and lying enemy. Be discerning, and ask the Lord to keep you from buying into his tactics of deceit.

Satan Divides

The deceit of Satan usually leads to division in some manner. Satan knows that anytime he can divide the troops, he has a greater likelihood of preventing God's work from being carried out. He will lie. He will scheme. He will do everything he can in order to bring division.

He will attempt to divide your heart away from your first love, Jesus. He will mislead you to buy into the world. He will mislead you to soak your life in career and future. If he is successful, you may want to serve God, but your interests have changed. You have been deceived!

Satan will attempt to divide your family. The conflicts in your family that end up in division in relationships between you and your spouse, between you and your children, between the children, or between relatives are all Satan's attempt to divide. He may bring division to your family through a simple fight, or even through divorce. He uses anything that divides. Do not be deceived by his tactics of division any longer. The next time you begin to sense that Satan is at work in your family, address the conflict for what it is. Inform everyone of Satan's tactic, and run away from getting caught in it.

Satan will attempt to divide your church. In every area of church life, he will attack with the strategy of division. If you and your church are in conflict right now, Satan is leading the charge. He may be disguised as something else, such as a building program, budget issues, or personnel issues, but rest assured that the enemy is leading the division. If your pastor and congregation are divided right now, it is occurring for one reason: Satan is behind it! God does not divide His people. This is only in the hands of Satan. Recognize Satan's tactics and refuse to be a part of his plan. Call it what it is with courage. Denounce it privately, publicly, and prayerfully. Declare with courage that you are not going to let Satan divide your church. Take actions for repentance, reconciliation, and restoration.

Satan Destroys

The ultimate goal of Satan's strategies is destruction. Satan does not play games; he plays for keeps.

Satan is involved in every drug deal. He is involved in every murder. He is involved in every school shooting. He is involved in every divorce. He is involved in every erotic video or Internet site. His ultimate goal for you is destruction.

Satan wants to destroy you. He wants to end your effectiveness or your life, preferably both. His goal is to see your testimony destroyed or your mouth shut about the things of God. If he has already lost you for his kingdom through salvation in Christ, he has to use you in some way to bring destruction or to destroy you.

Satan wants to destroy your family. Do not let him do that. His eye is on your marriage. His eye is on your children. His eye is on your happiness. He wants to bring to a total end what you would perceive as family today. He is the one who has perverted the definition of family in our culture. He has now made all sorts of things acceptable in the minds of the masses so he can further his plans among us.

Satan wants to destroy your church. He hates the church that has a heart for the Great Commission. He hates the church that has a pastor who proclaims the full counsel of God with courage. He hates the church that puts people in the streets to help the hurting people in the world. He will do all he can to destroy these kinds of churches. Yet Satan does not mind churches that preach an easy Christianity in which you drop in one hour a week and get your "religious needs" filled. He is not threatened by a church that does not think evangelism is important. In fact, when he finds churches that are committed to easy Christianity and have little or no commitment to sharing the gospel, he will even help fill them. It just adds to his strategy of deceit to make people think they have something when in reality they do not. Satan is in favor of anything that destroys the gospel going into the entire world.

Be informed. Satan deceives, divides, and destroys. There is no easy path in life when you are following Jesus with all of your heart.

Be informed. Satan deceives, divides, and destroys. There is no easy path in life when you are following Jesus with all of your heart.

Conflict Within Yourself

When your heart is burning with fire for the Lord, you will also experience inner conflict. The Bible speaks to this in Galatians 5:16–17: "But I say, walk by the Spirit, and you will not carry out the desire of the flesh. For the flesh sets its desire against the Spirit, and the Spirit against the flesh; for these are in opposition to one another, so that you may not do the things you please." This conflict is with your flesh.

Your flesh represents the "natural man," using the terms of Scripture (see 1 Cor. 3:1). The natural man desires to fulfill his own desires. He lives for himself at every turn.

The Spirit is the Holy Spirit. The Holy Spirit comes to live within your life upon conversion.

When the Holy Spirit comes to live within you, you will experience immediate conflict. The flesh sets itself against the Spirit. The Spirit sets itself against the flesh. The battle rages between the two. The battle is to see whether your will or God's will wins in the decisions of life.

This opposition is not a personality conflict or chemical imbalance. It is intense warfare between your flesh, which leads you toward selfish desires, and the Holy Spirit, who leads you toward God's will.

Your only hope for victory is to understand that your old flesh is dead. You are now alive unto God! The desires of the flesh lead to carnality and death. The Spirit leads to life and peace. The key to victory is to be controlled by the Holy Spirit of God. Letting Him lead you will result in spiritual victory.

Just remember, the more your life burns with fire for God, the more you will experience warfare with your flesh. Satan does not like the things of God, and neither does your flesh. Your flesh will rise up, trying to preserve its rights. The major problem is that it is impossible to walk with God while claiming your rights.

Yield your flesh to love God and to do God's will. You can overcome the conflict by being controlled by the Holy Spirit of God.

Conflict with the World

When your fire is burning for God with great intensity, you will face conflict with the world. The world and all it contains is not from the Father. First John 2:16 says, "For all that is in the world, the lust of the flesh and the lust of the eyes and the boastful pride of life, is not from the Father, but is from the world." Everything in the world is in conflict with God and His will. When you set your life to live for the Lord, you will experience conflict with the world.

The world has its own values and standards. These are not in line with God's Word. No worldly values and standards are from God.

Therefore, when you determine in your heart to live for God, burning with a great fire for God, you will face major conflict in the world. The reason for this is that the values of God and His Word run against the grain of this world. They are opposed. They conflict just like flesh and Spirit. The values of the world move into conflict with the values of God.

This is why the values of the so-called religious right are ridiculed by the intellectual elite and political pundits. Our values as Christians are radically different from the world's. Getting along with the world is unacceptable. The values of this world are opposed to God and His Word.

Therefore, when your fire burns for God, you will face spiritual conflict with the world. It will not count you as a friend, but as an enemy.

Conflict in the Church

The world's values have infiltrated the American church. The church prides itself on its corporate mentality and technological expertise. Churches are racing to see who is on the front end of change. Christian leaders read the books of the world and inject their secular principles into the body of Christ. The operation manual for the American church is now the most recent trend in the world that can be adopted and then blessed with a little bit of Jesus.

Why would the church want anything from the world? Please consider that question for a moment before racing toward the next sentence. Why would the church want anything from the world? That is a good question.

The church on fire for God will be radically different from the world. The church on fire for God will create major disruption in the American culture.

This is the reason that major evangelistic efforts in cities are considered hostile and intolerant. This is also why many churches face legal actions for property acquisition and building advancement. The church is in conflict with the world.

Let me also inform you that there will be conflict within the church when the Lord is active in the body of Christ. When the people of God are burning with fire, they will experience contention

> Let me also inform you that there will be conflict within the church when the Lord is active in the body of Christ.

within the church. There will always be people in the church on guard against God's movement in the church. It threatens their position and their influence. They do not understand it because they are lost or very carnal. There will always be people in the church guarding traditions and attempting to preserve the old wineskins that are brittle and inflexible.

A true movement of God will disrupt the church's structure, tradition, and status quo. Sadly, spiritual growth does not come easily within the church.

Stand for God and His ways in your church. Proclaim the truth-
fulness of the Word. Do not let mere men stand in the way of God.
Carnality is unacceptable to God, and it should also be unacceptable
to the church. Ironically, when God really begins to move, one of the
greatest battlefields may be in the church.

I have identified the four major conflicts you will face when fire
burns within. You will have conflicts with Satan, within yourself, with
the world, and within the church. Know they are coming, because
they *will* come. Let the actions you take be the actions the Lord and
His Word will be honored by in every situation.

OVERCOMING CONFLICT

You will experience many conflicts when you live for the Lord. The
question of great importance is, Can you overcome these conflicts? I
believe the answer is yes, and I want to show you how. There are three
steps of actions I want to motivate you to take to overcome spiritual
conflict.

Be Aware

Be aware that spiritual conflict is coming in your life. Understand
it is going to be a part of your life on a regular basis when you live for
the Lord. Recognize this conflict for what it really is.

If the conflict has a questionable source, creates confusion, divides
in any way, or is destructive in nature, know it is from Satan. You
must be aware enough to recognize it for what it is. If the conflict is
within you, be aware it is your flesh moving into conflict with the
Holy Spirit. If the conflict is with the world, see it for what it is. You
are simply going against what the world is all about. If the conflict is
within your church, you know immediately it is a battle with Satan
over the destruction of your church. Only he would divide the church
of Jesus Christ. Only he would lead someone who proclaims to be a

Christian to stand opposed to the work of the Holy Spirit. Therefore, recognize these conflicts. Be aware of them. They are coming.

Be aware that you are in a spiritual war. It is a very serious time. The peace of your own soul, the souls of others, the soul of your family, and the soul of your church are at stake.

Be Prepared

You need to be prepared for these conflicts. The evil days around you are critical days of satanic attack and trials. Therefore, you must be prepared to enter battle.

A United States soldier moving into battle in the Vietnam War was prepared. He had completed boot camp with success and taken numerous actions to prepare for war. He went into the battles of Vietnam with the needed armor and artillery. Thank God for our great soldiers, especially for those who gave their lives for our country.

Just as a soldier marched into battle in Vietnam prepared for battle, you need to march as a Christian prepared for battle. God has given you spiritual armor for battle. This battle is discussed in Ephesians 6:14–17:

> Stand firm therefore, having girded your loins with truth, and having put on the breastplate of righteousness, and having shod your feet with the preparation of the gospel of peace; in addition to all, take up the shield of faith with which you will be able to extinguish all the flaming arrows of the evil one. And take the helmet of salvation, and the sword of the Spirit, which is the word of God.

These verses describe your means of preparation for battle. You are to put on the full armor of God.

You are to gird your loins with truth. The loins are the middle section of your body. This is where your major sexual organs are located. God calls us to protect this section of our bodies with truth. When you gird your loins with truth, your life will be characterized by sexual purity.

You are to put on the breastplate of righteousness. This piece of armor protects your body from the shoulders to the loins. It protects your heart and other vital organs. God's righteousness and holiness are distinctive features of God. His righteousness is granted to you in Jesus Christ. Cover the vital part of your life with the righteousness of Jesus Christ.

You are to shod your feet with the preparation of the gospel of peace. The gospel of peace is the heart of Jesus' message. When Jesus is in your life, His peace serves to move you quickly in warfare and to make a difference for Jesus Christ. As you share the gospel, you will overcome your conflict.

You are to take up the shield of faith. This shield was estimated to be two and a half feet by four and a half feet in diameter. When a soldier was in a kneeling position, his entire body could be protected. Faith in the Lord and His teachings serves as your shield of protection. This powerful shield of faith can deflect even the flaming missiles of Satan.

You are also to take the helmet of salvation into conflict. The head is always a target in battle, but a helmet will protect it. One of the fiercest battlefields in the Christian life is your mind. Impurity, doubt, and discouragement will bombard your mind. Yet, your salvation is eternally secure. This helmet is one of salvation, safety, and assurance.

Finally, you are to take the sword of the Spirit, which is the Word of God. This is the only offensive weapon in your spiritual armor. The most powerful and proven weapon you have as a Christian is the Word of God. It is powerful! Use it in conflict.

This is the way you get prepared. Dress yourself every day with the armor of God in prayer. Put it on your family members in prayer. You are in serious conflict. Be prepared for the conflict by putting on the full armor of God.

Take Action

You cannot sit on the sidelines and let someone else fight for you in the battle of conflict. You are going to have to move toward action. If conflict goes away, it is only a sign that you have compro-

> You cannot sit on the sidelines and let someone else fight for you in the battle of conflict. You are going to have to move toward action.

mised your faith. Therefore, you want to take the needed action to overcome the conflict.

Take action in prayer. Prayer is the means by which you stand against Satan. Prayer is where the battles are won or lost. Since prayer leads you to the power of God, pursue taking action in prayer.

In my book *How to Pray*, I dedicated an entire chapter to warfare praying. I would strongly urge you to get that book for this one chapter alone. It describes specific ways to take action in prayer against Satan, the flesh, and the world.[1]

I want to urge you to take action in building relationships. When you walk with God, burning with a fire, your relationships will be tested because they become a target for Satan. Therefore, beat him to the punch and spend the necessary time to build relationships.

Satan will attack some of your closest relationships, so start there. Do everything you can to go the extra mile, bringing people along on spiritual things and preparing them for conflict.

I believe it is also very important to do everything you can to bring a resolution in every relationship. Do what you can do to bring peace, but not peace at any price. You should never sacrifice the things of God for anything or anyone. Yet your heart needs to resonate with a desire for repentance, reconciliation, and resolution.

There is no easy path when your life burns with the fire of God. When you face these inevitable conflicts, you can overcome them by being aware, prepared, and active in prayer, relationship building, and resolution.

CHAPTER 12

EXTREME CHRISTIANITY

The youth generation is a reflection of the American culture. Young people in the twenty-first century reflect the values and principles of the entire country. The present youth generation is extreme in every measure.

The youth generation is extreme in its sports. They no longer croquet on a sunny afternoon for fun; they jump out of airplanes, dive off of high cliffs, hang-glide, and skateboard in wild and crazy ways. This generation is turned on by extreme sports—sports that put you on the edge of life and death. Nothing is safe for this group when it comes to sports.

The youth generation is also extreme in its knowledge. They are learning things in junior high school that I didn't learn until I was in high school. They have grown up in the Information Age, and they are flooded with knowledge. They know things about life that some adults did not learn until they were well into marriage and family, things that are not always good for young people to know. With information accessible through television, radio, movies, books, newspapers, magazines, and the Internet, the youth generation is not short on knowledge at all.

The youth generation is extreme in technology. This is the generation in which most will be "techies" in order to survive. Many young people have their own computers or access to computers. The Internet is one of the most, if not the most amazing invention in recent years. It places the world and all its information at the fingertips of this generation. Many in this generation have their own cell phones and pagers. They have access to people, information, and the world at all times.

The youth generation is extreme in its clothing. Guys wear their pants as low as possible on their waists, and you will have to look a long while to see a girl wearing a dress. Both males and females wear rings not only on their ears, but their noses, lips, and tongues. Oh yes, I cannot forget to mention the hair. It is green, red, orange, blond, and styled according to the latest trend.

The youth generation is extreme in every way. In the year 1900, the average wage in America was three hundred dollars per year; the average teenager now spends that amount of money in three months. While there were only eight thousand cars in the United States in 1900, most in this generation own their own cars. In 1900, only 8 percent of the American households had a telephone, while many young people now have a phone in their own room. While there were only 230 murders reported in the year 1900, the American society is hoping that the next full year does not see as many teenagers and children shot on the campuses of their schools.[1]

The youth generation is extreme in every way. What does that mean to you if you are an adult? It means they are telling you about your culture. They are imparting to you that the entire country is extreme in many ways.

Everything in this culture is changing. It does not take twenty years to see change as it used to years ago. Now it seems that the culture changes every eighteen months or less. It is evolving into extremes as you have never seen in your life. It is not just a moral revolution any longer; it is a moral evolution that is always creating some new value in morality. This moral evolution has produced the popular idea that there are no moral absolutes. The absence of God's Word in the culture and the absence of real holiness in the church have created moral ambiguity and acceptability of all in America.

With the context of the American culture in your mind as you investigate this chapter, ponder the following questions.

THE QUESTIONS

The first question that must be answered is, *Why is the vast majority of the youth generation not drawn to Christianity?* This provocative question needs to be asked by every church, every pastor, every youth worker, and every youth pastor in America. It does not need to receive only a brief answer because it is critical to the future of America, your children, and your church.

The second question that must be answered is, *Why is the vast majority of the American population not drawn to Christianity?* This question needs to be answered with great thought by every pastor, church leader, and church in America.

The American population will continue to slide toward Gomorrah until these two questions are answered. I believe the same answer exists for both of the questions.

THE ANSWER

I am convinced that the reason our culture is not drawn to Christianity is that *the Christianity they see is not extreme enough for them.*

For an American culture that is extreme in sports, knowledge, technology, dress, and in many other ways, the Christianity they see is just not extreme enough for them.

> For an American culture that is extreme in sports, knowledge, technology, dress, and in many other ways, the Christianity they see is just not extreme enough for them.

They are not drawn to Christianity. They see few Christians living their faith. They see few Christians burning with a fire for God. When they visit churches, they see little to no excitement. The atmosphere is usually stately, cold, and unfriendly. In those churches in which they do see excitement, they wonder why this excitement is not effective in the lives of the Christians they know. They do not see authenticity and spiritual power.

Some churches are attempting to address this issue by duplicating what the world is doing. But when unbelievers visit this kind of church, they are puzzled as to why there is little difference in the lifestyle of their churchgoing friends and their own lifestyle. Even though it may feel good when they go, they do not hear much that will help them in their lives.

Every Christian in America needs a genuine walk with Christ that is being set ablaze with God's fire, resulting in extreme Christianity. The spiritual discipline of extreme Christianity will be very attractive to unbelievers when they see it exist in your life. Initially, they may not understand or appreciate it, but in God's timing it may be the very thing God uses to bring them to Himself.

Extreme Christianity does not mean you are obnoxious and babbling spiritual things continually. It does not mean you are offensive when you share your faith. Extreme Christianity does not mean you turn your church service into a pep rally. It never means you sacrifice the truth of the gospel in any way in order to appeal to more people. Extreme Christianity also does not mean you attempt to fabricate something into happening spiritually in your life or church.

I am not sure what extreme Christianity means to you, but I do want to give you some thoughts. Extreme Christianity means you are real. It means you go farther with Jesus than you have ever gone in your life. It means you reach spiritual heights that you have never reached before. It means you let God ignite a fire within you. It means you implement spiritual disciplines that will set your life on fire.

There is no reason to fear becoming an extreme Christian. God will lead you along the way as He does things in you that are incredible—within the context of your unique personality.

If you will move forward in your walk with Christ with a burning fire for Jesus and a deep burden for a lost world, you will be viewed as radical and extreme. Do not be worried about these tags. They are the badges of the Christian faith. Let me show you what I mean.

THE MODEL OF EXTREME CHRISTIANITY

One of the most exciting books in the entire Bible is the Book of Acts. It records the acts of the Holy Spirit in the church of Jesus Christ. The

Book of Acts reveals how God worked in the church within the first few years following the coming of the Holy Spirit on the day of Pentecost.

The entire book records how radical and extreme these Spirit-controlled disciples and churches were in the culture in which God had placed them. These Christians wore the labels of "radical" and "extreme" as honorable badges of the Christian faith.

One of the most exciting events recorded in Acts, which serves to capsulize what was happening in those first few years in Christians and in the churches, is found in Acts 17. Paul and Silas were ministering in the city of Thessalonica. They explained God's Word and gave evidence that Jesus was the Christ, the Son of the Living God. Many people were persuaded, including many Jews, to follow Jesus.

The Jews were very angry about these events. Some wicked men formed a mob and set the city in an uproar. The mob attacked the house of a man named Jason. They wanted to bring out Paul and Silas, as well as others who were causing such a stir in the city. They were not able to find Paul and Silas at Jason's house, but they dragged him out of his home and shouted at him.

I want you to notice the words recorded in Acts 17:6, referring to the disciples and followers of Jesus: "These men who have upset the world have come here also." The King James Version says, "These that have turned the world upside down are come hither also." The New International Version says, "These men who have caused trouble all over the world have now come here." The Message, a paraphrase version, says, "These people are out to destroy the world, and now they've shown up on our doorstep, attacking everything we hold dear!" After dragging Jason out of his home, the Jewish leaders accused him of welcoming these troublemakers who were saying there was another king other than Caesar, someone named King Jesus. After continuing the disturbance for a while, they released Jason. Later that evening, the brethren sent Paul and Silas away to Berea. Thessalonica was no longer a safe place for them.

Go back and consider what people were saying about these

Christians. They were called troublemakers. They were accused of upsetting the world. They were accused of destroying the world because they attacked the things people held dear. Friend, these were radical Christians.

They were radical in their commitment. They were extreme in their faith. They caused a stir everywhere they went because they were ablaze with the fire of God. They truly were world changers.

I am convinced that when America sees Christians who have that kind of radical commitment and extreme faith, America will come to Jesus. Being like the world attracts no one from the world, but being different from the world gains the attention of the world. If people see authenticity and consistency in the lives of those who live extreme Christianity, they will come to Christ in countless numbers. Then America will see another spiritual awakening across this great land.

> If people see authenticity and consistency in the lives of those who live extreme Christianity, they will come to Christ in countless numbers.

The Christians in the Book of Acts are our heroes in the faith. We study what they say; now it is time to live as they lived. They lived extreme Christianity.

WHAT WILL EXTREME CHRISTIANITY MEAN TO YOU?

When you begin to live with your heart set ablaze with the spiritual disciplines I have shared in this book, what will extreme Christianity mean to you?

Extreme Lifestyle

Extreme Christianity will mean an extreme lifestyle. Your faith will be so powerful that your whole life will be affected. Every area of your life will be influenced by your Christianity.

Many Christians see their lives as being very compartmentalized.

They work on Monday through Friday. They clean house, mow the yard, entertain guests, or play golf on Saturday. On Sunday, they go to church. They do not see any relationship of their Christianity to Monday through Saturday. Quiet honestly, the vast majority of people do not see their faith even affecting church on Sunday.

This is not extreme Christianity. The kind of Christianity God reveals in His Word impacts every segment of a person's life. It affects your lifestyle in every way. Nothing is untouched by your Christianity.

This extreme lifestyle will determine your attitude in life. You will stop seeing the glass half empty, but half full. You will begin to have the attitude of Jesus which He talked about in His Sermon on the Mount. You will begin living under the control of God's Spirit to such a degree that the fruit of Spirit will be your adornment. People will begin to see love, joy, peace, patience, kindness, goodness, faithfulness, gentleness, and self-control. Your attitude will be one of gratitude. Your entire disposition will change when you are living extreme Christianity.

This extreme lifestyle will influence your family life. Spiritual matters will become important in your family—not just on Sunday as they may be now, but every day. Love will permeate your home because you will be praying for your family. Things will change at your address when you begin living extreme Christianity.

This extreme lifestyle will determine your choices. Earlier in the book, you learned the valuable spiritual discipline that every choice is a God choice. Extreme Christianity will influence every choice you make. You will not make them in a flippant manner anymore, but you will consider God's will and His Word as you pray through them. Whether it is a choice in friendship, church, job, or priority, your Christianity will determine your decisions.

Extreme Purity

Extreme Christianity will lead you to extreme purity. You will exchange your mind for the mind of Christ every day. Your innermost desire will be purity.

Extreme purity will determine the movies you see. You will no longer sit quietly while your Christianity is violated by open immorality or ridicule. You will begin to rise from your chair in a gentle and inoffensive manner, speaking to someone in the theater to share with him or her the reason you are leaving. You may even ask for your money back, and you will probably get it.

Extreme purity will influence the type of places you tour on the Internet. This is a new major problem that Christians now face at an alarming rate. Open pornography sites, chat rooms for sensual talk, and other activities are causing a startling rise of immorality. Many Christians and their families are falling prey to the enemy. Extreme purity will lead you to protect yourself and the members of your family. Your computer records each Web site you or members of your family have viewed. It might be wise to learn how to check where everyone has been. You never know what happens when Satan leads to deceive. Extreme purity calls you to be concerned about the status of your purity both inwardly and outwardly.

> Extreme purity calls you to be concerned about the status of your purity both inwardly and outwardly.

Extreme purity will determine the purity of your dating life or the dating lives of your children. As a single adult, it is a very difficult challenge to remain sexually pure in this culture. Years ago, people married in their mid- to late teenage years. Today, people wait until their mid-twenties to early thirties to marry. Some beyond that. How do you stay pure? Be careful whom you date. Do not go out with non-Christians. Beware of dating carnal Christians. Choose to let your date know of your commitment to sexual purity until after marriage. If you are a parent of a dating child, guard your child's sexual purity with aggression. I can assure you that Satan is using someone to try to take it away.

Extreme Impact

Extreme Christianity leads you to make an extreme impact. It does not let you sit comfortably and satisfied with your influence any longer, but it pursues ways you can make an impact for Jesus Christ. Every Christian should impact his or her culture—not just a segment of it, but all of it.

Extreme impact needs to be made in the workplaces of America. Let the light of Jesus Christ shine through you on the job. Be a conscientious worker. Begin a Bible study during lunchtime in your workplace. Invite those who do not know Christ to the study. Become a prayer warrior for your coworkers. Let them know you want to pray for any needs they have. Demonstrate a great attitude in the workplace, never giving in to gossip or any form of insubordination.

You can make an extreme impact in your community. Do not sit on the sidelines during the activities of your children in their school. Become involved in various organizations so you can insert your Christian influence. Become involved in community civic clubs or community recreation programs. You cannot impact the community for Jesus when you only surround yourself with Christian friends and activities. Use your time wisely to impact your community.

Extreme impact can involve just one person. You never know the impact you can make with your life, as the following story illustrates:

Dr. Frank Mayfield was touring Tewksbury Institute when, on his way out, he accidentally collided with an elderly floor maid. To cover the awkward moment, Dr. Mayfield started asking questions, "How long have you worked here?"

"I've worked here since the place opened." the maid replied. "What can you tell me about the history of this place?" he asked. "I don't think I could tell you anything, but I could show you something."

With that, she took his hand and led him down to the basement under the oldest section of the building. She pointed to one of what looked like small prison cells, their iron bars rusted with age, and said, "That's the cage where they used to keep Annie."

"Who's Annie?" the doctor asked.

"Annie was a young girl who was brought in here because she was incorrigible—which means nobody could do anything with her. She'd bite and scream and throw her food at people. The doctors and nurses couldn't even examine her or anything. I'd see them trying, with her spitting and scratching at them. I was only a few years younger than her myself and I used to think, 'I sure would hate to be locked up in a cage like that.' . . .

"I didn't know what else to do, so I just baked her some brownies one night after work. The next day I brought them in. I walked carefully to her cage and said, "Annie, I baked these brownies just for you. I'll put them right here on the floor, and you can come and get them if you want. Then I got out of there just as fast as I could because I was afraid she might throw them at me. But she didn't. She actually took the brownies and ate them.

"After that, she was just a little bit nicer to me when I was around. And sometimes I'd talk to her. Once, I even got her laughing. One of the nurses noticed this and she told the doctor. They asked me if I'd help them with Annie. I said I would if I could. So that's how it came about that every time they wanted to see Annie or examine her, I went into the cage first and explained and calmed her down and held her hand. Which is how they discovered that Annie was almost blind."

After they had been working with her for about a year—and it was tough sledding with Annie—the Perkins Institute for the Blind opened its doors. They were able to help her and she went on to study and became a teacher herself. Annie came back to the Tewksbury Institute to visit, and to see what she could do to help out.

At first, the director didn't say anything, then he thought about a letter he'd just received. A man had written to him about his daughter. She was absolutely unruly—almost like an animal. He'd been told she was blind and deaf as well as "deranged." He was at his wit's end, but he didn't want to put her in an asylum. So he wrote here to ask if we knew of anyone—any teacher—who would come to his house and work with his daughter.

And that is how Annie Sullivan became the lifelong companion of Helen Keller. When Helen Keller received the Nobel Prize, she was asked who had the greatest impact on her life and she said, "Annie Sullivan."

But Annie said, "No, Helen. The woman who had the greatest influence on both our lives was a floor maid at the Tewksbury Institute."[2]

One person can make a difference. You are that person! Extreme Christianity leads to making an extreme impact with your life. You have one shot. Make a difference! Change your world!

> Extreme Christianity leads to making an extreme impact with your life. You have one shot. Make a difference! Change your world!

Extreme Church

Extreme Christianity leads to an extreme church. What a blessing it would be in America to have a reputation like that of the first-century church—a people with accusations that they are troublemakers in the city, turning the world upside down! I long to hear those words said about the American church.

Does this type of Christianity impact your church? Perhaps not, but it should. The fire within you should be so ablaze that God will use you in a profound manner in your church. Go to your pastor and share with him that you are ready to stand with him to turn your city upside down. Share with him your commitment to the success of his ministry, the church, and God's kingdom in your community. Set aside time to pray and work with him to lead the church to make an impact upon the pagan culture in America.

Christians are sick and tired of lukewarm and status-quo Christianity. They are discouraged when they attend church and think that it has no impact upon their lives and culture. They are looking for something radical and extreme. Something bigger than themselves. Something that only God can get the credit for.

You may think there is no hope for your church. But there is hope! Let me give you this challenge: *Rather than dumb down to church mentality, you need to step up to the call of Christ to extreme Christianity.*

Do not backslide in your faith in order to get along with the carnal Christians in your church. Step up to the claims of Christ, and in time they will see you are real. Your passion for Christ will be contagious. You may wonder what other people are going to say about you. Don't worry. They are probably saying something about you already. They might as well have something alive to talk about, rather than something lukewarm or dead.

Extreme Christianity leads you to an extreme and radical commitment to your church. Step up and be counted!

Extreme Future

Extreme Christianity also leads to an extreme future. God has fantastic plans for your life as you get into the flow of His Spirit. Your future really is as bright as the promises of God.

Extreme future may lead to the unpredictable. You never know what God may choose to do with you. He may transition you to another city. He may lead you to change jobs. He may even lead you to a different career.

God may even call you to give some time to advance His gospel around the world. Perhaps you could use a week or two of your vacation time to travel on a mission project in America or overseas. God may want you to give those days to your local church for ministry or to be an impacting counselor at youth or children's camp. God may even call you into the ministry. He may ask you to leave where you are and what you are doing for the purpose of entering into full-time Christian ministry. Be willing to do God's will if He calls you to go. Until you do, you will not be happy. You cannot run away from God's call into ministry.

A Call to Extreme Christianity

I am issuing a call for you to be a part of a new generation of Christians who will live extreme Christianity. I believe this call is from the heart of God to the American church. In order to make the greatest impact on the American culture, a new generation of Christians—young and old alike—must live extreme Christianity. Whoever has the ear to hear God's call, leave where you are and pursue God's call to extreme Christianity. This is the hope for revival and spiritual awakening in America.

This new generation of Christians who live extreme Christianity are going to be able to do so only as their lives are set on fire. Does the fire of God within you need renewal? Practicing the spiritual discipline of extreme Christianity will ignite your life! You will move into a new dimension of your relationship with God in which He will demonstrate Himself through you with the supernatural power of the Holy Spirit of God. This is the heart of this book. Heed the call. Enter your spiritual Promised Land.

Join me in being a part of this new generation of Christians who will live extreme Christianity. I am not going back to where I used to be. I am going to go with Jesus farther than I ever been before.

Come and go with me.

CHAPTER 13

OTHER FUEL FOR THE FIRE

There are times when you desire the flame to burn brighter in your life, but you need to come at the flame in a different way. As I came nearer to the deadline for this book, I felt I needed to come at the message in a different way. I did not want this book to be like other books in the marketplace. I was convinced that God wanted to raise this book up to make a major difference in Christians in America and across the world.

Even though I knew the general direction of the book, I was struggling with how to relate the message on the printed page. I was struggling with the structure of the book, which usually comes very easily for me. I was also struggling with a very busy schedule and too few days that I could set aside for complete concentration for this writing project. It was a tough time, and the pressure seemed to be growing.

I pursued God about it daily. I prayed about what I needed to do and how I needed to do it. I felt that God did not want this message to stay in the warehouses and on the shelves of bookstores, but He wanted it in the hearts of His children. I knew God was going to have to do something extraordinary for me to be able to do what I sensed He wanted to do. I just did not know what it was.

Early one morning, I felt that God wanted me to tackle this writing project in a different way—not only in structure and writing format, but also in spiritual preparation and direction. I felt God wanted me to come to the flame from a different way. This would be different from any other book I had written. My heart grew with excitement, but I did not know how God wanted to do that.

The Lord soon confirmed to me that He was up to something very special with this book. It was again confirmed while listening

195

to Dr. Jerry Falwell preach a convocation service on the campus of Liberty University. My heart stirred when he preached a sermon entitled, "You Have Not Because You Ask Not." I knew God had me there to hear that message as I prayed about how this book needed to be written.

The clarity came while I was praying and reading God's Word. The Lord issued a call to fast and pray while writing this book. He spoke to me from Exodus 32 and 34:

> Then Moses turned and went down from the mountain with the two tablets of the testimony in his hand, tablets which were written on both sides; they were written on one side and the other. The tablets were God's work, and the writing was God's writing engraved on the tablets. . . . It came about when Moses was coming down from Mount Sinai (and the two tablets of the testimony were in Moses' hand as he was coming down from the mountain), that Moses did not know that the skin of his face shone because of his speaking with Him. So when Aaron and all the sons of Israel saw Moses, behold, the skin of his face shone, and they were afraid to come near him. (Exod. 32:15–16; 34:29–30)

On that morning, I felt that the Scriptures on those pages reached up and grabbed me. It was very clear to me that the Holy Spirit had given me this Scripture passage to show me how He wanted me to develop the book.

I do believe what you are reading from the beginning to the end of this book is the message of God for your life. No, it is not like the Ten Commandments that were written by the finger of God. But God can determine the impact this book will have on your life and on others.

I have felt led to pray in this focused time of fasting for three things about this book. First, that God would transform the life of every person who reads it. Second, that God would call out a new generation of Christians who would practice extreme Christianity through these disciplines. Third, that God would place within every reader the desire to share this book with a friend, a member of his or her family, or a member of God's family. This new generation can emerge when the call is issued through the reading of this book.

The message of reform has been ringing loud and clear through the 2000 campaign for the office of President of the United States. "Reform with results" is a penetrating message that catches my attention. In other words, you will not only talk about reform; you will see it and experience it.

This book is a message of reform with results. If you will let the Lord lead you through a time of spiritual reformation placing these disciplines in your life, you will see results in your life, the church, the nation, and the world.

Therefore, just as I had to be willing to come at the message of this book in a different way, there will be times in your spiritual life when you will need to come at the flame within you in a different manner. It will burn the embers deeper and enhance the power of the flame.

Other fuel for the fire include short-term, concentrated, and different ways to come at your flame within. These ways will provide new oxygen to the fire. They are methods that God might use to imprint these disciplines in your life. Are you ready for more fuel? I hope that God will use this other fuel to come at the flame differently in your life.

> Are you ready for more fuel? I hope that God will use this other fuel to come at the flame differently in your life.

OTHER FUEL FOR THE FIRE

Fasting

Fasting is one of the most neglected disciplines in the Christian life. Many Christians are ignorant of it because the American pulpit is silent about it. Yet, God's Word is clear about the power of fasting. Followers of God in the Old and New Testaments, including Jesus Christ, included fasting as part of their lives.

Fasting is abstinence from food with a spiritual goal in mind. Fasting is neglecting the body of the most natural thing it desires—food—in order to pursue the God of heaven to do something powerful in your life.

Why is fasting so powerful? Because it calls you to deny yourself. It calls you to crucify the flesh. It calls you to yield the members of your body completely to the Lord. Fasting is powerful because it calls you to the Lord so powerfully that food no longer satisfies you; you must be with Him to be satisfied. Fasting is also powerful because it calls you to withdraw a few extra moments from the world in order to be with God. I am not speaking of being a recluse, but I do believe some extra time with God, whatever that means to you, is the key to a powerful fasting experience.

I am often asked the secret of fasting. I believe the secret to fasting is obedience to God. As you initiate humility through your life by fasting, you are one of the few who are obeying God in this spiritual discipline. As a result of your obedience to God in self-denial, God pours His power upon your life in a supernatural way. God will answer your prayers more than ever before. He will move in this capacity not because fasting is a hoop you must jump through to get God's attention, but because fasting positions you spiritually to hear God speak to you, and it provides an amazing desire to please Him.

I have spoken at great length about the spiritual discipline of fasting in my books *The Power of Prayer and Fasting* and *How to Pray*.[1]

Would you begin to practice fasting? Consider whether God is calling you to a one-day, two-day, three-day, ten-day, twenty-one-day, or forty-day time of fasting and prayer. Of course, begin where you are. Do not leap into long-term fasting if you have not fasted before.

This spiritual discipline will be fresh fuel for the fire within. It is short-term, concentrated, and different.

Writing Scripture

In the second chapter of this book, I talked about the spiritual discipline of setting your life on fire with the Word of God. Writing God's Word can be a very refreshing spiritual exercise. When you discover a passage that is really meaningful to you, write it down, or type it into your computer. The specific concentration will force you to meditate upon the section of Scriptures. It will give you time to pray about it as you write it, thinking of ways God may want to use it in your life.

Listening to Scripture

The entire Word of God is available on audiotape. This can be a very refreshing exercise as you use your time well. You may have a brief or long commute to your workplace, but you can listen to Scripture before and after you battle with the pressures of work. This can be an effective stress reliever. While you are preparing for the day, you could listen to God's Word. When you are at home in the evening and have time for reflection, you could listen to God's Word. A prayer time coupled with listening to Scripture can be productive fuel for the fire within.

> A prayer time coupled with listening to Scripture can be productive fuel for the fire within.

Memorizing Scripture

I also mentioned memorizing Scripture in chapter 2. Do not neglect this important discipline. Few things in a moment of crisis can provide you God's wisdom any more than God's Word coming to you that you have memorized previously. Praying and memorizing Scripture can make the truth of God's Word come alive in your heart.

Praying Scripture

As I mentioned in chapter 2, praying the Word of God can be energizing to your devotional life. When God's Spirit really brings a passage home to you, pause and pray it to God. Personalize it while you pray it. Discover passages or sections of Scripture that the Lord wants you to pray through. At times, get on your knees while praying Scripture. It is refreshing!

Journaling

Journaling is the way you record God's activity in your spiritual life. It is one of the most powerful actions I have ever taken in my life.

Each day, I write a one-page prayer to God at the end of my quiet time. The goal of this written prayer is to record the burdens I am releasing to God, to write down scriptures God has used in my life that day, and to record my sense of my spiritual life. I begin my prayer with the words, "Dear God." I follow that by placing the day and time when I am writing the prayer.

There is power in writing these things down. There is a release that comes when you place them on the page. By doing this, you know that you really did give them to God.

Journaling is a great way to strengthen your faith. By recording God's activity in your life each day, you will be encouraged in days to come as you look back to see how God has moved in your life through prayer.

Personal Retreats

A personal retreat can be a great experience for you spiritually. It can be time alone in a cabin in the woods, a quiet hotel room, or any place of your choice. The purpose of this retreat is for you to get completely alone with God, without family, job, friends, or other things that can distract you in your spiritual life.

Take the Word of God, a journal to write in, and other things you feel you need, such as other Christian books or tapes. Be sure you keep the Word of God central in that retreat.

This spiritual retreat could be just overnight or a more extended stay. Private time with God is very important. When you need a fresh wind from the Spirit, a retreat can help you.

Mission Trips

A mission trip can be a very refreshing adventure for you. It can be a time where you really live your faith by rolling your sleeves up and working. On a true mission trip, you will be able to share the gospel and see God bring many people to repentance. You may even see a church planted from your work.

Denote your vacation time or part of your vacation time to a mission experience. Some of those can be in the major inner cities in America, regions of America where God is not known, or even overseas in a foreign land where the gospel is really good news to the people.

A mission trip gives you the opportunity to be a part of something much bigger than yourself or your church. It can be very fulfilling and rewarding for you spiritually. It is a great new way to come at the flame in your life.

Holy Land Tour

One of the greatest and most powerful things I have ever done is travel to Israel. Standing in the very places where Jesus lived and walked made the Bible come alive to me. There is nothing like being in the house of Caiphas, the place where Jesus spent the night before His crucifixion; the Garden of Gethsemane, where Jesus agonized in prayer; the Mount of Megiddo, where that great last battle will happen in the Valley of Armageddon; or the empty tomb where Jesus was raised from the dead. You can count a Holy Land tour as an investment in your spiritual life.

Conferences or Seminars

Many Christian conferences and seminars are available across the country. Attending a conference or seminar can be a very effective way to grow spiritually by coming at the flame in a different way.

Confer-ences and seminars are concentrated segments of time, usually from one day to three days. Some may even go for five days.

Identify your specific need and then attend a conference or seminar you believe will assist in that need. Remember, a conference or seminar is only as good as the leader. Ensure he is the kind of person God can use to ignite your life spiritually.

Spiritual Growth Plan

A spiritual growth plan is a specific strategy to implement in a segmented time of your life. For example, you may want to include a Bible-reading plan, tapes you want to listen to, Christian books you want to read, or interviews you may want to conduct with other Christians.

The plan could be for a one-year period of time. The year does not have to begin on the calendar year. The plan could be a thirty-day plan or whatever length of time you decide. Whatever the time frame, be reasonable about what you place in this plan. Do not overdo it. It is to be a time that motivates you, not a time you dread because you have encumbered yourself with too much to do. Set attainable goals for yourself.

A spiritual growth plan is only a track you run your spiritual life on during this segment of time. It is not where the power is. God still has that role in your spiritual life. Consider a spiritual growth plan—it may be just what you need to ignite your life.

> Consider a spiritual growth plan—it may be just what you need to ignite your life.

A New Thing

Pray and consider doing something new in your spiritual life. Something that you have never done before. Something that will stretch you. Something that will make you go farther than you have ever been with Jesus. It will get you out of your spiritual comfort zone and the rut that is so easy to endure. Let the Lord give you a new thing to do. It can be another refreshing way to come at the flame within.

Stop for Fuel

Do not wait until your spiritual tank is almost empty or totally empty to stop for more spiritual fuel. This can be very hazardous to your spiritual life. Stop for fuel soon. Use one of these concentrated and focused types of fuel over a short-term period of time. Using the right fuel at the right time can take your spiritual life to a new and exciting level.

Each one of these kinds of fuel can help set your life on fire. They will complement the spiritual disciplines from the previous chapters that God wants to graft into your life. As you graft them one by one into your life, they will set your life on fire.

CHAPTER 14

WHEN THE FIRE GOES OUT

A smoldering fire has more smoke than fire. With each passing moment, the embers wane. The flames are so low that they are barely noticeable. The conditions dwindle in such a way that the fire eventually goes out.

Is your spiritual life like a smoldering fire, marked more by smoke than fire? If so, your spiritual fire is going out. Have you neglected important spiritual disciplines in your life? If so, the embers of these disciplines are now turning to ashes. Is your faith becoming unnoticeable to others? If so, you have let the spiritual conditions of your life dwindle so that your spiritual fire is almost gone. Your fire is only as powerful as the spiritual condition of your life. A real fire is totally dependent on the surrounding conditions—

> A real fire is totally dependent on the surrounding conditions—weather, materials, and care.

weather, materials, and care. Your spiritual fire is just as dependent on the spiritual condition of your life. Your attitude is like the weather; if it is poor, your fire will be greatly hampered. Your spiritual disciplines are like the materials; if you have not grafted these practices into your life, there is little to nothing to burn. The care is like the attention given to the regulation of the fire; if you have neglected your spiritual life, your fire is smoldering at best.

Is it too late to save the fire from going out? It is never too late. Since your fire may be smoldering at best, you must take action immediately.

You are not alone. I have been right where you are many times. I have been able by God's grace to renew the fire within, and the Holy Spirit wants to assist you in doing the same.

The purpose of this chapter is to help you diagnose your spiritual condition and to prescribe some actions you need to take to ignite your life again. The questions will be personalized, so read them as if you are asking them of yourself. The actions will be specific but brief. Let's begin with the diagnostic questions.

WHY DID MY FIRE GO OUT?

I hope you will honestly and specifically address the question, "Why did my fire go out?" These provocative follow-up questions will help you discern the real reasons your fire went out.

Have I neglected having a meaningful time with God?

If you have neglected your spiritual life, your time with God has probably been inconsistent, ineffective, and irrelevant. You cannot accomplish successful Christian living without a meaningful time with God. Inconsistency, carelessness, and negligence will result in the fire going out.

Do I have any unconfessed sin in my life?

Unconfessed sin leads to careless living, and it quenches and grieves the Holy Spirit of God. Unconfessed sin also interrupts fellowship with God. If you continue in unconfessed sin, you will extinguish your spiritual fire.

Am I holding on to a specific sin in my life?

Sin is attractive and sometimes it is difficult to let go and repent of it. As long as you do not get caught, you feel pretty good about it, but you know attempting to manage your sin is not pleasing to God. God hates sin. He does not want to share you with anything, especially sin. A refusal to repent of your sins results in the fire going out.

Do I have a relationship that is not right?

A broken or strained relationship threatens your spiritual life. If more than one such relationship exists, you are in the spiritual emergency room in need of immediate care. A strained or broken relationship is sin, which will result in your fire going out.

Did I lose focus in my life? If so, when? What caused me to lose my focus?

When you are distracted, you lose focus in your spiritual life. If the fire is waning, you are out of focus. Something is getting your attention and energy more than God is. It is important for you to know when you began to lose your focus. Pinpoint the moment or the experience. Seek specific things that may have caused you to lose your focus so you will not make the same mistake again. Losing focus in your life always plays a part in your fire going out.

Before you race on to complete the book or to return to chapter 2, take the necessary time to answer the questions listed in the above section. Stop suppressing your spiritual growth. It takes time to walk with God and to let your fire grow into a burning blaze. Before going forward, be certain you know the specific answers to the above questions. When you have worked through those questions in God's timing, then read on to the prescription to use when the fire goes out.

ACTIONS TO TAKE WHEN YOUR FIRE GOES OUT

When your fire goes out, you need to take the following seven actions immediately. In fact, if you implement these actions, you can prevent your fire from going out.

Honestly Answer the Above Questions

Take the time to answer the questions in the first section of this chapter honestly. As already stated, do not rush the process. If necessary, take a personal one-day retreat to reflect on these questions. It could become a great day of renewal for you. You would not have to rush the process. You could take the time needed to write down the answers to the questions.

A proper prescription is only effective based upon a proper diagnosis of the problem. Please be honest in answering the questions. God knows if you are being honest. Since He is the only One you are walking with spiritually, use integrity in the process.

Commit to Focus on Your Spiritual Life

You cannot renew the fire within until you make a new commitment to focus on your spiritual life. Other things may be pressing on you greatly, but nothing is more important than walking with God daily.

Set aside a segment of time daily to bring your spiritual life into immediate focus. Make the commitment to God. Be consistent in your commitment. When it is time to give focused attention to your spiritual life, do so. It is vital to your entire success. As your spiritual life goes, so goes the rest of your life.

Make Sure Your Heart Is Clean Before God

Identify any unconfessed sin in your life. Agree with God about its devastating effect upon you. Make a list of the sins you have recently committed. Ask the Holy Spirit to reveal them to you. Be sure to list the sins you are struggling to repent of in your life. These are the sins you seem to be confessing to God regularly. When the list of sins is complete, go back through each one, confessing them to God and receiving Jesus' cleansing blood upon each one of them. When you have completed this exercise, claim God's forgiveness by claiming a specific scripture like 1 John 1:9 or Psalm 51. Stand in that forgiveness. Receive the filling of the Holy Spirit in your life now that your sins are confessed, repented of, and forgiven.

When you sin again, do not let the sins pile up as trash. Confess them to God and ask to receive the filling of His Spirit again. Remember, confess and be filled.

Nothing will dampen and extinguish the flame of the fire quicker than sin. It is destructive to your spiritual fire.

Ensure Your Relationships Are Restored

As you identify all strained and broken relationships, take the initiative to make them right. Own the sin in the relationship. Do not blame anyone. You should have never let that relationship get in the condition it is in at the present time.

Go to God in prayer, asking His forgiveness. Jesus taught that forgiveness toward others precedes God's forgiveness toward you.

Then go to the person, asking his or her forgiveness. If you have been the person who caused the relationship to be strained or broken, tell him or her you have sinned against

> Regardless, if the relationship is strained or broken, you are responsible for restoring it.

God. If the other person initiated the problem, say, "I am here because God convicted me that our relationship is not right. I must have sinned against you, so please forgive me. Will you forgive me?" If the person has sinned against you, he or she may immediately confess that he or she was the cause of the problem, not you. Regardless, if the relationship is strained or broken, you are responsible for restoring it.

Make Sure Your Time with God Is Meaningful and Daily

Plan your day around your time with God, rather than planning your time with God around your day. Diligence in preparing for this time is essential to a successful time. Be diligent to have the time orderly so that your attention will be on God, rather than having to fumble for the right things necessary for a meaningful time with God.

Be just as diligent to spend time with God daily. Since you live daily, you need to walk with God daily. Plan a specific time every day to have an appointment with God. Just as you would not break an important appointment, do not break this appointment with God. Make the commitment to Him that you will do it.

Resolve to Practice Extreme Christianity

Be a part of a new generation of Christians who will live extreme Christianity. This brand of Christianity is radical and extreme—the type of Christianity exhibited by first-century Christians when they were known as troublemakers who turned the world upside down.

Be a part of a new generation of Christians who will return to this kind of Christianity—the kind that is so different from the world that it is attractive to them.

Join me in calling other Christians to be a part of this new generation of world changers that are ready to turn the world upside down. Resolve that you will be a part of this new generation and that you will actively bring others with you.

Apply the Spiritual Disciplines of This Book into Your Daily Life

If you do not graft the spiritual disciplines of this book into your daily life, your fire will only be temporary. These spiritual disciplines are the deep embers of your spiritual fire. They are the substance for your walk with Christ.

Devotion alone will run out. But spiritual disciplines are the substance to your devotion. They are continually burning embers that will make you burn longer and hotter for God than ever before. When devotion and spiritual disciplines are combined, your life will become a combustible fire that will never go out.

When you graft these spiritual disciplines into your life daily, your fire will blaze. Each one of these disciplines is significant to your spiritual success. Work through them one at a time. When these disciplines are operating simultaneously in your life, you will have a life with deep embers and blazing fire!

MY FINAL WORDS

I asked you in the first chapter if you wanted to go on a journey with me to higher ground. If you are going to return to chapter 2, then the book is before you. If you have made it to this point all the way through the book, I want to thank you for joining me in the journey. You are now equipped to live on the highest spiritual plane.

There will be no more smoldering ashes and smoke for you. A life of deep embers and a blazing fire is God's plan for you. Do you still want to see fire? Graft these spiritual disciplines into your life, and you will develop deep embers and a blazing fire.

When you have truly experienced *Life on Fire*, your life will never be the same. These spiritual disciplines will ignite your spiritual life. Without them your future is bleak. With them your future is God-sized!

Life on Fire is the journey for a lifetime!

NOTES

Chapter 2: Setting Your Life on Fire

1. Warren W. Wiersbe, *The Bible Exposition Commentary, Volume 1* (Wheaton, Ill.: Victor, 1989), 279.

Chapter 3: Making God Choices

1. D.C. Talk and the Voice of the Martyrs, *Jesus Freaks* (Tulsa: Albury Publishing, 1999), 136.
2. Ibid.
3. Ibid., 137.
4. Ibid.
5. Sources for the life of Polycarp included D.C. Talk and the Voice of the Martyrs, *Jesus Freaks,*136–38; Kenneth Scott Latourette, *A History of Christianity Volume 1* (San Francisco: HarperCollins, 1953), 81, 130–31; and W. H. C. Frend, *The Rise of Christianity* (Philadelphia: Fortress Press, 1984), 126, 133–34, 138–40, 143, 156–61, 212–13, 230–31, 241, 256.

Chapter 4: Early, First, or Nothing

1. Ronnie W. Floyd, *How to Pray* (Nashville: Word, 1999), 29–44, 211–22.

Chapter 6: Rescuing God

1. Ronnie W. Floyd, *Choices* (Nashville: Broadman & Holman, 1994), 3–5.

Chapter 7: Worship That Changes the Rules
1. Ronnie W. Floyd, *The Power of Prayer and Fasting* (Nashville: Broadman & Holman, 1997), 2–5.

Chapter 8: Exchanging Your Mind
1. Charles Swindoll, *Maybe It's Time . . . To Laugh Again and Experience Outrageous Joy* (Nashville: Word, 1992), 79–80.

Chapter 9: Finding Your Oak
1. Jamey Ragle, sermon delivered at First Baptist Church of Springdale, Arkansas, 27 February 2000.

Chapter 10: Faith in the Fire
1. Warren W. Wiersbe, *The Bible Exposition Commentary, Volume 2* (Wheaton, Ill.: Victor, 1989), 318.

Chapter 11: No Easy Path
1. Floyd, *How to Pray*, 127.

Chapter 12: Extreme Christianity
1. Leigh W. Rutledge, *When My Grandmother Was a Child* (New York: Dutton Publishing, 1996), 130.
2. "One Person Can Make a Difference," e-mail sent by Kenneth Uptegrove, Springdale, Arkansas, 2 March, 2000.

Chapter 13: Other Fuel for the Fire
1. The author's *The Power of Prayer and Fasting* (Nashville: Broadman & Holman, 1997) is a very extensive book on the subject. In *How to Pray*, there is a chapter devoted specifically to fasting, entitled "How to Empower Your Prayers."

My Deepest Appreciation

No book is ever written without the help of many people. I would like to thank:

Gayla Oldham, my personal assistant and friend, who finalized this manuscript to present to the publisher;

Anita Stewart, my staff blessing and friend, who accompanies Gayla on grammatical and structural insights of the manuscript;

Tommy Hinson, my colleague in ministry and friend, who gave me insights along the way on this subject and project;

Greg Johnson and Chip MacGregor of Alive Communications, who dreamed this project with me and envisioned its potential influence upon others;

Mark Sweeney and Word Publishing for believing in me and the message that God has placed in my heart to share with the world;

Jeana Floyd, my wife for life, who sacrificed greatly during this project of time with me and service t me while I fasted and prayed for forty days while writing this manuscript;

Josh and Nick Floyd, my two sons and heroes, who are striving to live for God in this Christless culture;

John and Elva Floyd, my parents who raised me in the Lord and His Church, who celebrated their 50th Wedding Anniversary on March 10, 2000; Fred and Effie Thomas, my parents-in-law and colleagues in pastoral ministry, who on October 13, 1999, were separated physically by Fred's death after 56 years of marriage;

and to our Wonderful Lord Jesus Christ, who sustained me by His Spirit in my most intimate journey with Him while writing this manuscript.

ADDITIONAL RESOURCES

BOOKS

- *Reconnecting,* Broadman & Holman Publishers, 1993
- *Choices,* Broadman & Holman Publishers, 1993
- *The Meaning of a Man,* Broadman & Holman Publishers, 1996
- *The Power of Prayer and Fasting,* Broadman & Holman Publishers, 1997
- *How to Pray,* Word Publishing, May, 1999

RESOURCES

- www.lifeonfire.com
- *God's Gateway to Supernatural Power: A Resource, Testimony and Practical Guide on Prayer and Fasting,* LifeWay Christian Resources, 1996.
- *How To Pray* video series, Thomas Nelson Publishers, October, 1999.
- *Invitation to Life,* TV ministry of First Baptist Church, Springdale, Arkansas. National television broadcasts on Fox Family Channel, Odyssey and FamilyNet.
- www.fbc-springdale.org, First Baptist Church, Springdale, Arkansas Internet website. Listen to live Internet broadcast each Sunday morning at 9:30 A.M. (CST), learn more about this ministry and order products on-line.
- DayStar, Tape ministry of First Baptist Church, Springdale, Arkansas. Complete audio and video library of past thirteen years of Dr. Floyd's messages. For a complete listing of messages including series or specific subjects contact Daystar, P.O. Box 6970, Springdale, Arkansas 72766-6970 or (501) 751-4523.

MOST POPULAR SERIES

- Sex, Singleness, Dating, Marriage and Divorce
- Spiritual Warfare
- True Worship
- How Do You Love God?
- The Mind of Christ
- The Forgiveness Factor